Dynamic Patterns
Visualizing Landscapes in
a Digital Age

T0266778

Dynamic Patterns
Visualizing Landscapes in
a Digital Age

Karen M'Closkey and Keith VanDerSys

Routledge
Taylor & Francis Group

LONDON AND NEW YORK

First published 2017 by Routledge

2 Park Square, Milton Park, Abingdon, Oxfordshire OX14 4RN
605 Third Avenue, New York, NY 10017

Routledge is an imprint of the Taylor & Francis Group, an informa business

First issued in hardback 2020

Copyright © 2017 Karen M'Closkey and Keith VanDerSys

The right of the authors to be identified as authors of this work has been asserted by them in accordance with sections 77 and 78 of the Copyright, Designs and Patents Act 1988.

All rights reserved. No part of this book may be reprinted or reproduced or utilised in any form or by any electronic, mechanical, or other means, now known or hereafter invented, including photocopying and recording, or in any information storage or retrieval system, without permission in writing from the publishers.

Notice:
Product or corporate names may be trademarks or registered trademarks, and are used only for identification and explanation without intent to infringe.

British Library Cataloguing-in-Publication Data
A catalogue record for this book is available from the British Library

Library of Congress Cataloging-in-Publication Data
A catologue record for this book has been requested

ISBN: 978-0-415-71132-6 (hbk)
ISBN: 978-0-415-71133-3 (pbk)

Typeset in Grotestque MT by Camille Sacha Salvador at Luke Bulman — Office

MIX
Paper from
responsible sources
FSC® C013056

Printed and bound in Great Britain by
TJ Books Limited, Padstow, Cornwall

Contents

Foreword by James Corner

This is a beautifully stimulating and important book. It speaks to pattern and process and expands our understanding of how patterns inform, shape, structure, and influence our world.

A quick perusal through the following pages showcases an amazing and alluring collection of images—a wide variety of patterns that are visually gorgeous, suggestive, and inspiring. At first glimpse, one might assume that this is simply a beautiful pattern book, a 21st-century version drawn from current advances in imaging technology, digital media, and representational innovation. The casual reader might be visually impressed but think that this is all about pattern in its most superficial reading, pattern as purely visual surface, seductively beautiful but of limited import for so many issues facing our society today.

Yet a closer reading, a more nuanced and careful reading of both text and image, reveals much deeper and profound values than simply surface gloss. M'Closkey and VanDerSys masterfully unfold the many layers and capacities of pattern. At stake are some of the most fundamental of human concerns—relationship, connection, structure, allusion, possibility, innovation, and experience. This book speaks to how we as humans see, conceptualize, interact, value, and innovate. It speaks to art, science, technology, design, and humanism. More specifically, it speaks to how people relate to their environment, to the physical world of experience, and perhaps most profoundly and deeply, to the world of the *other*, to the world we do not yet know, the still to be discovered and found, experiences and effects yet to be made, hidden in patterns still to be disclosed.

Patterns are relational frameworks that simultaneously describe and project; they *reveal* structures, processes, and relationships, as well as *structure* physical frameworks that give shape and form to our world. Think of a trans-continental flight looking down upon the patterns of the earth in which dendritic hydrological patterns formed as small tributaries join larger streams and rivers and larger volumes of water accumulate and shape the land; graded outwashes and braided textures reflect rapid floods and dissipation of water; grids and lines lend order to settlements and land use. These various patterns are tied into the processes that shape them, as well as them-selves forming the physical conduits, pathways, and networks for energy, materials, and forces to actually flow and interact. Patterns are dynamic, active, and always working—distributing, assembling, binding, coalescing, connecting, and so on. They speak to ecology and nature as much as to aesthetics, human invention, and representation. By extending our understanding of pattern into the digital world, M'Closkey and VanDerSys remind us of the generative and hidden forces of pattern, the diagrammatic and representational structures that give rise to new understandings, new forms, and new possibilities.

The authors show how pattern can be both instrumen-tal (patterns perform work) and disruptive (patterns suggest alternative readings, disrupting convention and habit). The authors also show how patterns affect mood and experience, influencing psycho-somatic responses in an inter-connected eco-sphere. Patterns induce new types of emotion, connection, and response. In this way, the authors eloquently argue for a dialogue, or even a synthesis, among appearance, performance, and aesthetic reception. Here, pattern is not simply graphic but also and at the same time fundamental for both influencing and shaping processes and potentialities that are at once mate-rial and perceptual, physical and psychic. Such reciprocity helps to meld the scientific mind with the artist, at once both measurably explanatory and immeasurably illuminating.

Finally, it is important that this book on pattern is tied quite specifically to landscape architecture: to an enhanced understanding and analysis of landscapes, as well as to actually imagining, projecting, and inventing new forms of landscape. Here, the crux is not simply new patterns and forms for their own sake, but rather new patterns and forms that structure new ecologies, new programs, and new modes of reception.

Our world is an ever-evolving kaleidoscope of dynamic patterns, each structuring relationships and modes-of-being; this book provides thoughtful and suggestive insight into how patterns work and their value for our very humanity.

Preface

Dynamic Patterns: Visualizing Landscapes in a Digital Age explores the role of patterns in contemporary landscape design. We examine methods that foster a multivalent understanding of patterns as both the expression and shaping influence of environmental processes. The importance of patterns for landscapes is not a recent development; nevertheless, patterns are ripe for reinvention in light of current environmental preoccupations and in connection with recent techniques enabled by digital media.

Although digital media are pervasive, little attention has been paid to the effects of these media in the shaping of landscape expressions and forms. Publications on this topic in the field of landscape architecture often take the form of software-based technical manuals or collections that are categorized by drawing type. A number of recent publications suggest that this gap is beginning to be filled, and we hope that our book makes an additional contribution.[1] It is important to note, however, that *Dynamic Patterns* is not an argument for the use of any one particular tool or medium over any other. This book appeals to readers to think about digital techniques as means of calculated discovery that can open up design possibilities through exploration and experimentation. Techniques, whether in design, science, or any other area of inquiry, have always inhabited a realm between useful "fiction" and material reality. It cannot be otherwise; our understanding of the world is fused with the methods that we use to represent it.

While there are innumerable ways to interpret and explain landscapes and environments, our central focus is on various tools and techniques that enable us to see and create patterns. This book has drawn inspiration from many sources, but two thinkers are of particular note: the polymath Gregory Bateson and the artist György Kepes. Both Bateson and Kepes argued for the importance of pattern recognition as the central mode by which to engage environmental relations.[2] They were writing and practicing at a time when system thinking was emerging as a powerful conceptual framework. Although this framework originated over seventy years ago, it has continued to evolve and has taken on renewed relevance as our tools for visualization have become more powerful. For this reason it is worthwhile to look back at what these thinkers considered to be the opportunities and drawbacks of this framework. For example, Bateson warned that the increasing positivism associated with the systems thinking of his day—valuing only that which can be quantified or measured—will never lead us out of our environmental predicaments. Designers are increasingly asked to substantiate their work through "metrics," however, these criteria alone do not encompass the full value of landscapes. The pattern recognition that Bateson and Kepes argued for, which must of course continue to evolve in order to remain relevant to today's contexts, is first and foremost an aesthetic framework, which is ultimately what our book is about. Aesthetics is not a superficial or "extra" concern that shrouds more fundamental issues or realities; it is the means by which we come to understand them.

Book Organization

The introduction outlines the importance of systems thinking and ecology to landscape architecture and describes the centrality of pattern with respect to these broader frameworks. We then describe specific instances of how patterns have been employed recently in landscape architecture. The subsequent chapters utilize a selection of work from various practices and are organized around three themes—topological patterns, behavioral patterns, and ornamental patterns—that address the affiliation between pattern and process in distinct ways.

Chapter 1, *Topological Patterns*, explores how processes that influence form and organization in the designed landscape are geometrically and parametrically measured and modeled. This chapter critiques the limited use in landscape architecture of digital media—often restricted to functioning as a surrogate for hand-drawn techniques—and describes how digital media facilitate the use of information to structure relationships. The projects highlighted in this chapter show the ways in which the organization of data, including relationships among different datasets, can bridge between pattern-finding and pattern-forming.

Chapter 2, *Behavioral Patterns*, frames patterns in temporal rather than geometric or formal terms. Given the speed and level at which we humans now manipulate our environment—and ourselves—distinctions between organic and synthetic, natural and artificial, or animal and human are increasingly difficult to maintain, thus creating the need for frameworks that are not based on such dichotomies. Because patterns are relational rather than categorical, they can contribute to this reframing. The projects highlighted in this chapter, which are related conceptually to early systems art, use pattern recognition to bridge spatial and temporal scales, thereby linking real systems and abstract systems (digital signs).

Chapter 3, *Ornamental Patterns*, considers the question of symbolic form and critiques the supposed divide between utilitarian and symbolic functions. This chapter examines how new modes of visualization have facilitated the formation of patterns that both *invoke* and *evoke* animate characteristics —that is, patterns that conjoin ornament (as icon or representation) and organicism (as morphological and functional organizations). The projects in this chapter offer fresh interpretations of landscape processes in response to today's environmental contexts by framing material processes, sustainability mandates, and functional criteria with overtly stylized and representational forms.

As will hopefully become evident in the following pages, *Dynamic Patterns* is not a "how-to" pattern book, nor does it make any claims for a universal or comprehensive form of pattern. Instead, we follow Kepes's intention, which is to use a visual argument to create "a book of allusions not conclusions."[3]

Introduction

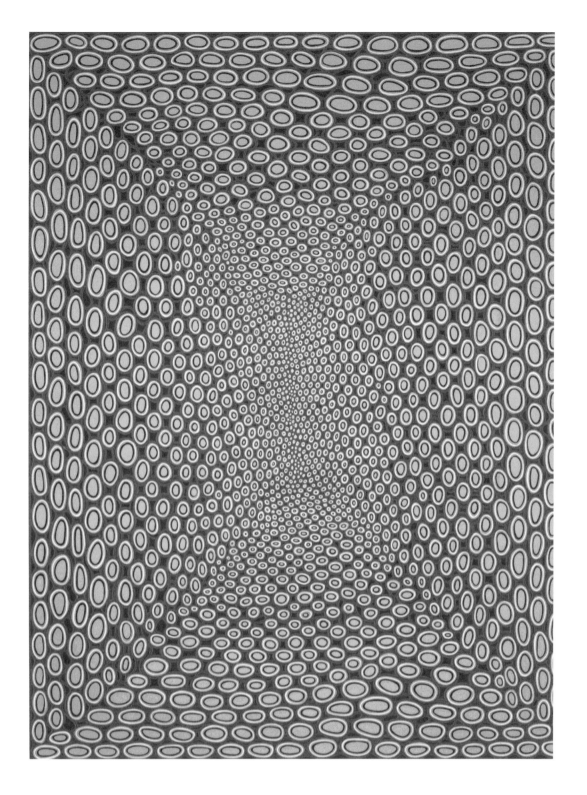

1. James Siena, *Battery*, 1997, enamel on
aluminum, 74cm x 57.8cm.

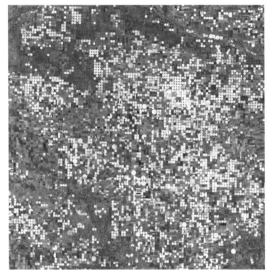

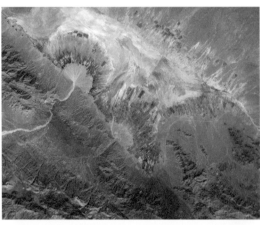

Patterns in designed landscapes are often understood as implying the imposition of order, reflecting human dominance over the complexities and flux of nature. At times they are equated with static surfaces, such as parterres and paving patterns; in other instances they are associated with the repetitive configurations of urban or agricultural land use. Yet the importance of patterns goes well beyond such readily recognizable formal attributes as simple surfaces or uniform geometries. Patterns—formal, material, or temporal recurrences— are essential for perception. Humans have an innate ability to recognize patterns; our brains are wired to perceive them and to seek them if they are not immediately visible. We look for patterns in nature in order to understand relationships between function and form, as in morphology, and between information and communication, as in genetics. Patterns are synonymous with processes; they are indications of the forces and interactions that created them. Since many designed landscapes are constructed interpretations of nature that are physically embedded in living processes, patterns have enduring relevance for landscape architecture both representationally and materially. As our knowledge of nature changes, our depictions of nature change correspondingly. The inverse is also true; that is, the tools and techniques used to measure and represent natural processes lead to changes in how knowledge is produced. Visualizations made possible through computation and digital imaging have provided new tools for understanding and depicting these processes. This being the case, a primary aim of *Dynamic Patterns* is to elaborate upon how various design techniques, especially those enabled by digital media, have facilitated different ways of seeing and making patterns and thus new ways of understanding landscapes and designing our place within them.

In our positioning of patterns, we seek to provide a framework for interpreting various projects that are emblematic of a broad shift in sensibility over the last few decades. This shift involves a diverse constellation of influences and ideas that derive from wide-ranging and differing interpretations of ecology. This gathering of ideas has led to an increase in

2. Satellite image, Garden City, Kansas.

3. Satellite image, agriculture within an alluvial fan, Zagros Mountains, Iran.

4. Hubble Space Telescope image of the M101 galaxy. Highly complex and repetitive structures are found across scales, from the macroscopic spirals of galaxies to the microscopic helixes of DNA.

Introduction

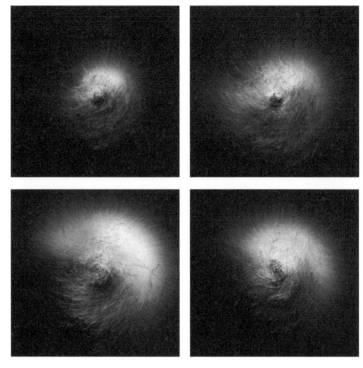

5. Mark Nystrom, *Wind Process 2015.01*. The wind series uses custom algorithms to plot collected wind data. In this instance, the plots start from a center point and then are "pushed" away from the center based on wind conditions at the time of data collection; for example, faster winds move the point a greater distance from the center while winds from the west push the point to the right. A location for the next second of the day is determined and a series of lines are drawn between the two points. This process continues until twenty-four hours of data have been interpreted.

what might be called an "ecological consciousness."[1] Thus another fundamental aim of this book is to focus on patterns as a primary means by which the rise in ecological consciousness has been expressed in thinking and methods associated with design.

Although ecology as a science originated in the late nineteenth century, it did not become broadly popular as a conceptual framework until the 1960s and 1970s, when it began to be used to denote holistic thinking. This expansive understanding of ecology has further increased in recent years to encompass ongoing efforts to engage with larger environmental concerns. There are many ways to think ecologically, including by considering natural systems in land use planning; by developing "green" technologies; by paying attention to social-environmental interrelations across scales ("think globally, act locally"); or by adopting an all-encompassing "ecology of mind."[2] These expanded interpretations of ecology beyond science *per se* are prevalent in the humanities and philosophy, leading some to argue that ecology is the most significant epistemological framework of our time.[3] Not surprisingly, the effects of ecological thinking on landscape architecture have been profound.[4] To be clear, this book is not about the science of ecology, the application of ecological principles to the management of large-scale landscapes, as in landscape ecology, or the quantifiable functions of landscapes, such as ecosystem services. That ground has been well traversed by others. Nevertheless, the various approaches to pattern-finding and pattern-forming that we see in design today cannot be understood apart from

6. Bridget Riley, *White Disks 1*, 1964, emulsion on board, 132cm x 132cm. The abstract patterns of Op Art produce perceptual effects whereby the surface of the canvas appears to flicker, pulsate, and move.

7. Emma McNally, *S24 (detail)*, 2009, hand-drawn graphite on paper, 100cm x 140cm.

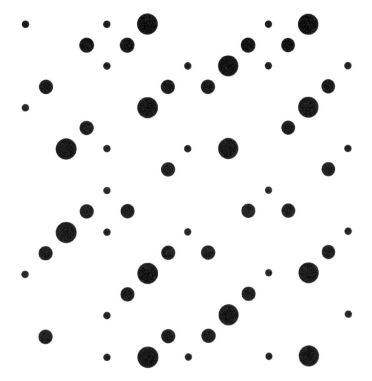

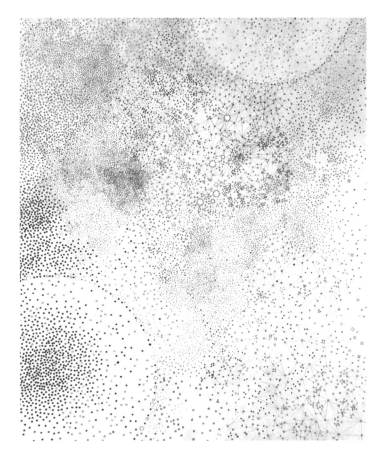

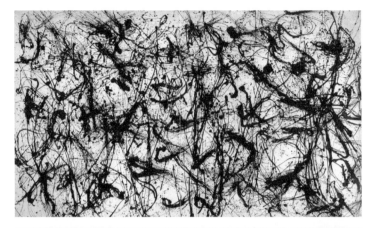

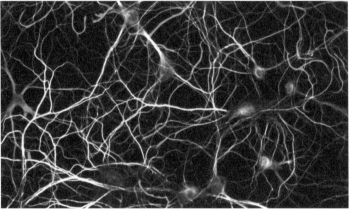

8. Jackson Pollock, *Number 32*, 1950, enamel on canvas, 269cm x 457.5cm, Museum of Modern Art, New York.

9. Image of cultured astrocytes, a type of brain neuron.

the influence of systems thinking, which entered into the discipline of landscape architecture largely through the field of ecology. For that reason, any discussion of patterns today must be rooted in a discussion of systems and ecology. The number of publications and diversity of scholars dedicated to examining systems thinking is profuse; here we will only briefly touch on the history and development of systems thinking in order to lay a foundation for explaining why this way of thinking has been important to landscape architecture and how patterns have been one of its primary manifestations.

If ecology and systems are common frameworks used to describe the constellations of relationships that we see in the world—the "what" of the world—then patterns are the "how," or the means by which we come to know, understand, or express these relationships. That is the focus of this book. As the title suggests, new forms of digital media are central to these explorations. Our focus, however, goes beyond any particular software, design technique, or drawing type; rather, we emphasize the ways in which patterns are used as vehicles to understand, describe, and convey environmental processes.

We chose patterns as our organizing principle for two additional reasons. First, patterns exist outside such categorical distinctions as nature versus culture, which most people agree are no longer tenable in our hybrid world. Like hybrids,

Dynamic Patterns: Visualizing Landscapes in a Digital Age

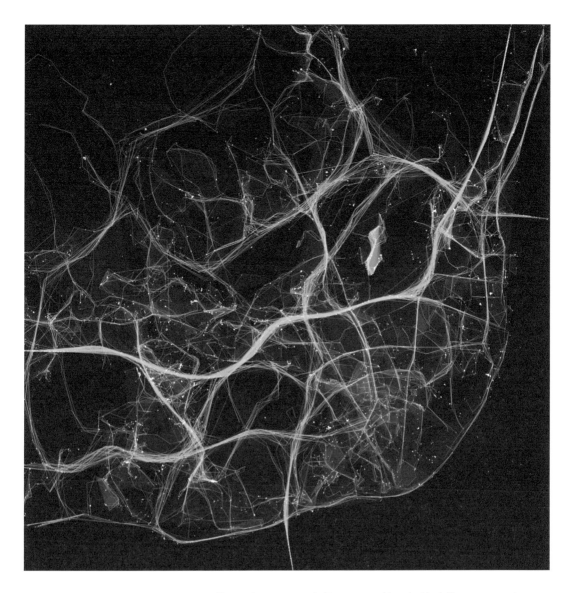

10. Pedro Miguel Cruz, Penousal Machado, and João Bicker, 2010. Visualization of traffic flow in Lisbon over a twenty-four-hour period through the GPS trails of circulating taxicabs. Line thickness and color represent traffic density and speed, respectively.

patterns have associative properties, in that they are made up of multiple entities; unlike hybrids, though, they do not result from a combination of previous classifications and therefore do not rely on such categorizations in the first place. Patterns do not exist in things themselves but only in relations between or among things. Second, patterns are inherent in the methods used to describe natural and artificial systems; therefore, they are specific to the theories underlying the philosophical and scientific developments that characterize systems thinking, yet broad enough to provide an overarching theme for looking at a wide range of methods and projects that employ patterns in distinct ways.

Systems Thinking

Systems thinking swept through the sciences, humanities, and arts in the early twentieth century and remains central to many disciplines.[5] A system consists of any number of entities that interact with each other within defined spatial or temporal boundaries. As systems theorist Donella Meadows explains, "There are no separate systems. The world is a continuum. Where to draw a boundary around a system depends on the purpose of the discussion."[6] Systems have also been defined as "any pattern whose elements are related in a sufficiently regular way to justify attention," or as a "set of elements or parts that is coherently organized and interconnected in a pattern or structure that produces a characteristic set of behaviors."[7] Systems theory arose from biology with the development of general systems theory in the 1930s to 1950s (by Ludwig von Bertalanffy), and it was simultaneously developed in mathematics and cybernetics (by Norbert Wiener) and ecology (by the Odum brothers). Cybernetics—the study of control and communication in systems—exerted a particularly profound influence on ecology. Though the concept of ecosystems existed prior to the inclusion of cybernetic thinking in ecology, the coalescing of the two helped ecology to become a dominant science. Eugene and Howard T. Odum, the veritable forefathers of ecosystem study, pioneered the use of a notational language to study system behaviors, illustrating material and energy flows as if they were parts of an electrical circuit.[8] The flows were diagrammed as gains and losses that represented energy and organisms moving into and out of a particular ecosystem. The use of circuits as analogs for describing feedback loops provided ecologists with a tool for modeling biological processes in ecosystems as a whole, regardless of scale. This ability to schematize the overwhelming complexity of interactions was widely adopted, though it soon came under scrutiny for its mechanistic and reductive view of nature.

Early influential thinkers, including noted anthropologist and cyberneticist Gregory Bateson (*Steps to an Ecology of Mind*, 1972), extended the concept of systems and ecology to

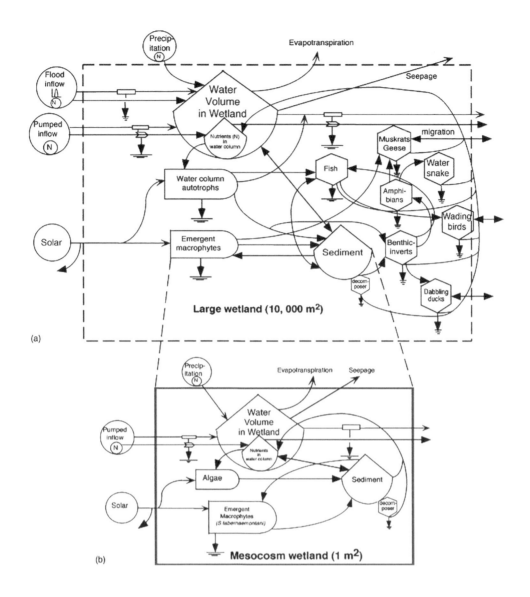

11. Howard T. Odum created energy
diagrams to model environmental
systems visually. The symbols denote
key characteristics of energy exchange
in biological processes—source,
loss, storage, production, and
consumption—and lines denote
pathways among these processes.
The diagrams were used to develop
mathematical equations for the system
under study.

include all human relations, especially the problem of human communication and communication media.[9] Bateson was concerned that interpreting ecology through a purely material paradigm of energy flow and exchange would result in a mechanistic and quantitative view of humans' relations to nature and to each other.[10] He believed that ecology must be understood in terms not only of its material order but also its communicative order, that is, by the "patterns that connect" everything together, to use his oft-cited phrase.[11] For Bateson, ecological consciousness and patterns are inseparable.

This more inclusive understanding of systems provided a conceptual framework for dealing with the interconnectedness of a rapidly changing world. The shift occurred concurrently with growing awareness of global resource depletion, increasing pollution levels, and mounting population growth. This multi-scalar and interrelated understanding of the world was aided by ecology, biology, and physics, not simply because of what scientists were discovering about pollution (e.g., Rachel Carson's 1962 classic *Silent Spring*) or projecting about future population trends (Donella Meadows' 1972 work *The Limits to Growth*), but because new methods, including advancements in optical tools and the incipient phases of computation, made it possible to portray the dynamics of an ever-changing world.[12] Newfound environmental consciousness, abetted by NASA photographs of the earth from outer space, changed our collective image of the planet as well as our sense of humanity's place within it, as best summarized by the then-popular expression "spaceship earth." This broadening of the meaning of ecology and systems to encompass social, mental, and political domains, all integrated with environmental considerations, is widely taken for granted today.[13] Yet there remains a great deal of ambiguity and disparity of intent among designers seeking to import ecological concepts and systems thinking into design. This is not a problem in and of itself, but it is helpful to distinguish the different aims prevalent among designers who pursue this approach.

13. Michael Batty, 2013.
The sequence of images shows the
result of an agent-based model
that simulates the growth of a city.

14. John Ruskin, c. 1860.
Ruskin recognized the power
of fractional geometric patterns
long before fractal geometry
was created.

Systems and Ecology in Landscape Architecture

In the 1960s and 1970s, ecological principles and systems became increasingly relevant to theories and practices of the designed environment, as seen in the work of landscape architect Ian McHarg and others involved in regional planning. McHarg's adoption of the thermodynamic model to describe living systems was very much informed by the Odums' work on ecosystems, in which energy flow and feedback maintain systems in dynamic equilibrium, thus illustrating nature in balance. In contrast, the influence of cybernetics on landscape architect Lawrence Halprin's work, as well as on that of many artists of this era, involved different means and ends. Halprin's approach offered a way to think about systems that was not limited to interpreting them through the lens of natural science.[14] Cybernetics uses feedback loops wherein an action or event generates a change in the environment that is then fed into the system, causing a change in the system, and so on in cyclical fashion. Halprin drew on this concept to create a method of fostering participants' engagement in interactive design workshops. As these early examples demonstrate, systems thinking in landscape architecture has been interpreted in diverse ways, not all of which include direct engagement with natural systems. In fact, the interpretation of science by landscape architects had, and often still has, little to do with the scientific method, which is experimental in approach and provisional in its conclusions. Rather, their interpretation involves borrowing scientific concepts and a rigorous methodology as a means to substantiate land use and management decisions, as in McHarg's case, or expanding the methods by which designers engage participants in their environment, as in Halprin's case.[15]

As scientific paradigms change, so too do their interpretations in the design fields, and, as the above examples show, scientific concepts are interpreted in quite different ways. As McHarg, Halprin, and their contemporaries were developing design methods inspired by cybernetics, major developments in the sciences and mathematics coupled with improved computer technologies were radically altering

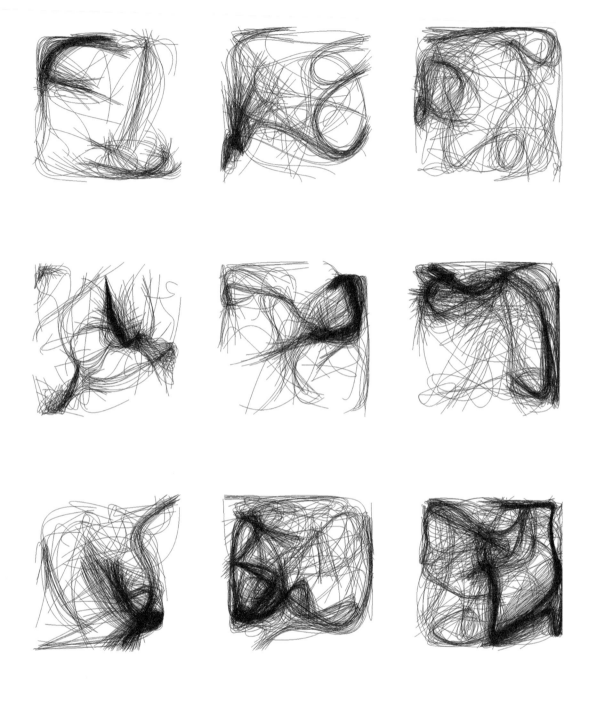

15. Hyun Chang Cho, 2008. Simulations using Craig Reynolds' flocking algorithm to visualize the aggregate motion similar to that of a murmuration.

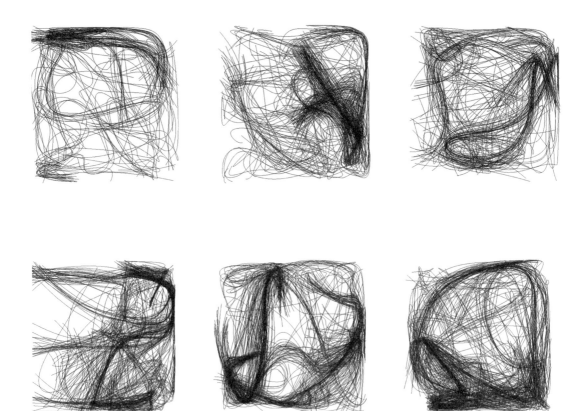

how the behavior of systems was understood. These developments led to the widespread study of self-organization and emergence, an approach that foregrounds the unpredictability and spontaneity of nature and represents a direct repudiation of the mechanistic view of nature in balance.

Emergent Patterns

The shift from viewing ecosystems in thermodynamic terms to understanding them as more open and unpredictable began in the 1970s and led to a redirection of researchers' emphasis away from looking for stable patterns in dynamic equilibrium to looking for emergent patterns in self-organizing systems.[16] According to physicist Fritjof Capra, a chief theorist of systems thinking, the theory of self-organizing systems is the broadest scientific formulation of the ecological paradigm.[17] Research on self-organization happened not only in the biological sciences, but also in mathematics and physics with the development of fractal geometry and chaos theory, both of which describe emergent behaviors. Fractals are self-similar patterns across scales, created by repeating a simple process in a feedback loop, which eventually produces complexity. Chaos theory, colloquially known as the "butterfly effect," holds that a small initial input in a non-linear system can lead to much larger and more complex effects over time. This emphasis on self-organization also contributed more generally to the use of ecology as a metaphor, not only for the relatedness but also for the mutability of all things, marking a philosophical shift from *being* to *becoming*.[18] As with early cybernetics, the scientific and mathematical discoveries of emergence in natural systems were extended to the study of social systems and to the collective behavior of both humans and animals, a topic that we will address more fully in chapter 2.

Emergence refers to the behavior of complex natural systems, as well as to the computational modeling of such processes. The increased modeling capacity of computers was critical to the advancements taking place in all scientific and mathematical fields of study. The ability to model emergent behavior was well established in these fields by the time these ideas made their way into design thinking, an event that coincided with the infusion of computers into design schools in the early to mid-1990s.[19] With these preoccupations came new departures in how patterns were understood and created. In architecture, for example, interest in emergent patterns in nature has inspired wide-ranging formal expressions, such as bio-morphology, or resemblances between human-made structures and natural structures, and emergent form, which uses genetic algorithms to "grow" formal variations from fixed parameters.

In landscape architecture, by contrast, emergence generally does not refer to formal variations produced during the design process but to material and cultural transformations that are presumed to occur *after* design implementation. As ecologist and planner Nina-Marie Lister notes, "A systems-based perspective of living systems rests on the central tenets of complexity and uncertainty, and necessitates flexibility, anticipation and adaptation rather than prediction and control in conservation planning and management."[20] Likewise, James Corner states that "a truly ecological landscape architecture might be less about the construction of finished and complete works, and more about the design of 'processes,' 'strategies,' 'agencies,' and 'scaffoldings'—catalytic frameworks that might enable a diversity of relationships to create, emerge, network, interconnect, and differentiate."[21] This notion of emergence presumes that, once the initial conditions have been set in place, ecological processes will unfold and the landscape will evolve toward a state of greater complexity.

A seminal moment marking the permeation of contemporary systems thinking into landscape design was the competition held for Toronto's Downsview Park in 1999. The framework for this competition drew explicitly on systems theory, and the notion of emergence formed the basis of several of the schemes selected as finalists. Julia Czerniak highlights

17. Henry J. Oosting, Laurentian Shield sphagnum bog succession diagram. Reprinted in Lawrence Halprin, *RSVP Cycles* (1969).

18. James Corner Field Operations, *Fresh Kills*, Staten Island, NY, 2001. Habitat phasing diagram.

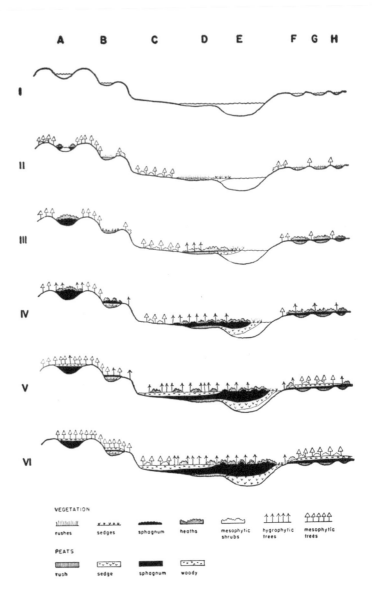

HABITAT PHASING

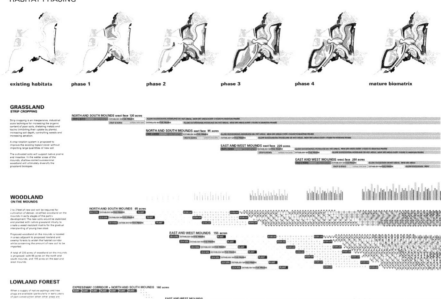

existing habitats   phase 1   phase 2   phase 3   phase 4   mature biomatrix

GRASSLAND
STRIP CROPPING

Strip cropping is an inexpensive, industrial scale technique for increasing the organic content of poor soils, chelating metals and toxins (inhibiting their uptake by plants), increasing soil depth, controlling weeds and increasing aeration.

A crop rotation system is proposed to improve the existing topsoil cover without importing large quantities of new soil.

The cultivated soils will support native prairie and meadow. In the wetter areas of the mounds, shallow-rooted successional woodland will ultimately diversify the grassland biotopes.

NORTH AND SOUTH MOUNDS west face 130 acres

NORTH AND SOUTH MOUNDS east face 95 acres

EAST AND WEST MOUNDS east face 220 acres

EAST AND WEST MOUNDS west face 260 acres

WOODLAND
ON THE MOUNDS

2 to 3 feet of new soil will be required for cultivation of denser, stratified woodland on the mounds in early stages of the park's development. The new soils would be stabilized and planted with native grassland initially to create a weed-resistant matrix for the gradual interplanting of young tree stock.

Proposed woodland on the mounds is located in areas adjacent to proposed lowland and swamp forests to widen the habitat corridor while conserving the amount of new soil to be imported.

A total of 220 acres of woodland on the mounds is proposed—with 65 acres on the north and south mounds, and 155 acres on the east and west mounds.

NORTH AND SOUTH MOUNDS 65 acres

EAST AND WEST MOUNDS 155 acres

LOWLAND FOREST

When a supply of native saplings and tree plugs are available (particularly in early years of park construction when other areas are being prepared for planting), lowland and swamp forests are planted in overlapping woodland bands on existing soil to build the woodland rim.

EXPRESSWAY CORRIDOR + NORTH AND SOUTH MOUNDS 160 acres

EAST AND WEST MOUNDS

YEAR   1   2   3   4   5   6   7   8   9   10   11   12   13   14   15   16   17   18   19   20   21   22   23   24   25   26   27   28   29   30   31   32   33   34   35   36   37   38   39   40

19. Stan Allen and James Corner Field Operations, *Emergent Ecologies*, Downsview Park, Toronto, 1999. Planting strategy.

20. Bernard Tschumi/Dereck Revington Studio, *The Digital and the Coyote*, Downsview Park, Toronto, 1999. Planting succession diagram.

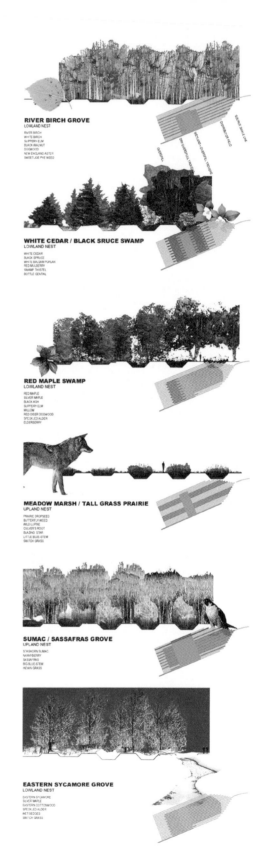

RIVER BIRCH GROVE
LOWLAND NEST

RIVER BIRCH
WHITE BIRCH
SLIPPERY ELM
BLACK WALNUT
DOGWOOD
NEW ENGLAND ASTER
SWEET JOE PYE WEED

WHITE CEDAR / BLACK SRUCE SWAMP
LOWLAND NEST

WHITE CEDAR
BLACK SPRUCE
WHITE BALSAM POPLAR
RED MULBERRY
SWAMP THISTEL
BOTTLE GENTIAL

RED MAPLE SWAMP
LOWLAND NEST

RED MAPLE
SILVER MAPLE
BLACK ASH
SLIPPERY ELM
WILLOW
RED OSIER DOGWOOD
SPECKLED ALDER
ELDERBERRY

MEADOW MARSH / TALL GRASS PRAIRIE
UPLAND NEST

PRAIRIE DROPSEED
BUTTERFLY WEED
WILD LUPINE
CULVER'S ROOT
BLAZING STAR
LITTLE BLUE-STEM
SWITCH GRASS

SUMAC / SASSAFRAS GROVE
UPLAND NEST

STAGHORN SUMAC
NANNYBERRY
SASSAFRAS
BIG BLUE-STEM
INDIAN GRASS

EASTERN SYCAMORE GROVE
LOWLAND NEST

EASTERN SYCAMORE
SILVER MAPLE
EASTERN COTTONWOOD
SPECKLED ALDER
WET SEDGES
SWITCH GRASS

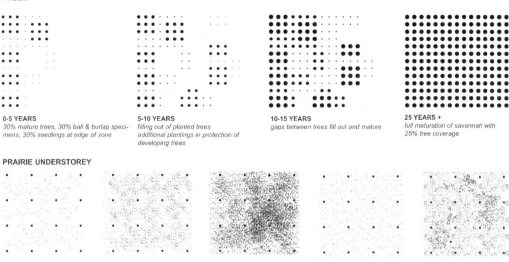

TREES

0-5 YEARS
30% mature trees, 30% ball & burlap specimens, 30% seedlings at edge of zone

5-10 YEARS
filling out of planted trees
additional plantings in protection of
developing trees

10-15 YEARS
gaps between trees fill out and mature

25 YEARS +
full maturation of savannah with
25% tree coverage

PRAIRIE UNDERSTOREY

year 1
plant plugs & seed mix away
from trees

year 2
praine grasses & annauls emerge

year 3
perennials emerge

year 4
quadriannual burning of
understorey

year 5
cycle begins again

this fact in the introduction to her book *Case: Downsview Park Toronto*, in which she argues, "Emergence refers to the development of detectable patterns in information and belongs to both ecological and cybernetic theory."[22] In some of the proposals for the competition, such as those submitted by the teams led by Field Operations (*Emergent Ecologies*) and Bernard Tschumi (*The Digital and the Coyote*), patterns of growth and change were represented in phasing diagrams that illustrated a shifting landscape over time. The Field Operations scheme in particular relied on the repetition of similar ridges and furrows that would give rise to diverse habitats depending on their different water quantities, soil conditions, and maintenance regimes. This project exhibited the potential for patterns to demonstrate difference through the use of formal repetition, while remaining open to change through environmental interaction. In positioning its project, the team did not explicitly address this goal of difference within similarity in terms of what specific effects it might wish to convey, stating, "Geometry and form is [*sic*] less important for what it might mean or look like than for what it actually does."[23] The designers were primarily concerned with emergence as a material property of natural systems rather than with the perceptual differences that might arise from such processes. Although different habitats were illustrated as part of the design, it was unclear what particular relationships were structured among these habitats and whether it would matter if they did not evolve as represented—if, for example, all ridges and furrows evolved into very similar habitats or if they did not exhibit increasing plant and animal diversity.

The concept of emergence encompasses the notion that social systems are similar to natural systems, in that they evolve in unanticipated ways and thereby thwart our ability to plan their future development with any definitive ends in mind. This notion of emergence suggests a more bottom-up and flexible approach to design than that which master plans could be expected to offer. The winning Downsview Park scheme, *Tree City*, led by OMA/Bruce Mau, took this view of emergence to an extreme by proposing a diagram that was a-spatial, a-formal, and a-material. The designers simply recommended the quantities and types of programs that should occur, without any specificity as to where they should occur. The crucial design elements needed to support the potential evolution of the park, such as grading and planting, were neglected in favor of managerial organizations out of which the project would eventually evolve. In this example, systems thinking and its affiliated terminology of self-organization and emergence were interpreted in such a way as to equate the absence of a design "product" with indeterminacy and flexibility. In other words, this view of systems looked only at potential social organizations and not at formal and material ones or the potential relationships among all of these realms. Although one might argue that this approach challenges aesthetic norms by not providing any specific formal or spatial outcomes, the plan that resulted from this process was, unsurprisingly, a banal and uninspired landscape.[24] In other words, it challenged such norms by default and not through engagement with them, unlike OMA's earlier and more compelling Parc de la Villette proposal.

As the winning scheme for Downsview Park demonstrates, one interpretation of systems thinking has been a de-emphasis on form based on the conviction that it is too fixed and cannot account for emergence in systems. It follows from such a view that issues of subjectivity and experience are secondary or perhaps impossible to ascertain.[25] This latter point is characteristic of a more general trend in landscape architecture today, wherein systems thinking has focused on large-scale networks and infrastructures, such as energy, waste, and transportation. This approach, where systems are understood

Park Program
Cultural Campus - Existing Buildings
Parking
Cultural Campus - New Buildings
WC/Information Centres/Security/Snacks
Recreational Water
Wetlands
Meadow Lots
Outdoor Theatre

mature park perspective:
Cooling off the kids at the
Six Pines Splash Pad.

mature park perspective:
Walking through the park
after the first Snow.

mature park perspective:
Running along the Locust
Lagoon path.

mature park perspective:
Meeting Space Exercise
studio.

mature park perspective:
Downsview Park Performance
at the Pope's Corner.

Site Context Plan

21. Bruce Mau Design Inc.,
Petra Blaisse, Inside Outside; and
Rem Koolhaas, Office for Metropolitan
Architecture, with Oleson Worland
Architects, *Tree City*, Downsview Park,
Toronto, 1999. Site plan.

principally in terms of functions or material flows that can be measured or optimized, has great relevance for comprehending urban or regional patterns. These considerations do not, however, preclude addressing systems through an aesthetic framework, as we do here. This book highlights the conspicuous aspects of a system—the points at which it can be understood as both a pattern of relationships and *experienced* as such. The difference between the two approaches is that, in large-scale networks, patterns are comprehended primarily through maps and drawings, whereas in many of the examples shown in the following chapters, the designers' intention is to build an understanding of patterns into the realm of experience beyond two-dimensional representations. Following the latter approach, a landscape's "ecological" or infrastructural functions are seen *in relation to*, rather than *in preference to*, their appearance and how they function as signs.[26] Implicit in this approach to patterns is the belief that sensory and aesthetic functions should play a much larger role in defining an ecological ethos for landscape design, as they did briefly in the 1980s and 1990s among theorists and landscape architects, and even earlier, as seen for example in Halprin.[27]

The emphasis on a landscape's operational aspects over its formal and expressive characteristics has not been limited to this recent interpretation of systems thinking; it is also true of various approaches that characterized landscape architecture in the 1970s and 1980s. We have already compared McHarg's adoption of a thermodynamic model for describing systems with Halprin's more open interpretation of cybernetics. The range of interpretations of systems and science among designers is broad, and their relevance should be understood within the context of individual projects and circumstances; unfortunately, they are often understood as dichotomous and incompatible approaches to landscape. Although such clear divisions as those between art and science or between qualitative and quantitative determinants are oversimplifications that exist only in rhetoric, this dichotomizing logic is perpetuated and infiltrates our field to this day, as other landscape scholars have noted. The landscape architect Sylvia Crowe, for

22. Panjin Red Beach salt marsh, Liaoning. The multi-colored zones are plants of the genus *Suaeda,* which turn vivid shades of red in autumn.

> 23. Myvatn Lake in Iceland is the result of a lava eruption that occurred over 2,000 years ago. These circular shaped pseudo craters resemble volcanic craters but lack a vent for magma.

example, who later co-authored *The Pattern of Landscape* (1988), defined landscape architecture in 1957 as a profession that aims to mend the "breach between science and humanism, and between *aesthetics* and *technology*" (emphasis added).[28] Likewise, Margot Lystra draws attention to the skirmish between Garrett Eckbo and Neil Porterfield in 1969–1970 in which Eckbo criticized environmental design approaches as suffering from "analysis paralysis," whereas Porterfield chided spatial designers as purveyors of "fantasy fatigue" who justified rearranging large areas of land by claiming artistic license.[29] Lystra quotes a similar statement by McHarg, who claimed that ecology offered emancipation to landscape architecture and that "the caprice and arbitrariness of 'clever' designs can be dismissed forever."[30]

In *The New Landscape in Art and Science* (1956), György Kepes cautioned against these distinctions, criticizing a perspective that, in his view, devalued art by positing that an entity's quantitative aspects are to be trusted because they are "real," whereas subjective and sensory experiences are to be suspected. Kepes argued that this "leads quite logically to a value judgment favorable to science and unfavorable to art."[31] On the contrary, the two realms are inseparable. Interpreting systems thinking primarily in terms of material and energy flows obscures the broader understanding of ecological consciousness called for by Bateson, Crowe, Kepes, and others. Patterns can bridge the divide between science and art by providing a link between material and experiential realms.

Analytic Versus Applied Patterns, or "Fitness" Versus "Flatness"

The above discussion has briefly sketched how systems thinking has been broadly interpreted in landscape architecture. In this section, a comparison between McHarg and Walker will help us to grasp more clearly how patterns have been employed in the recent past and how the latest forms of pattern both diverge from and build on these distinct approaches. Although the ideological differences between McHarg and Walker are clear and their practices are radically distinct, they share a key concern, in that an attention to pattern is evident in the methodologies of both designers. The use of new media can facilitate the recognition of connections between their two approaches to pattern, enabling pattern-finding while also making possible new kinds of pattern-forming.

      McHarg developed a systems approach to land-use planning, studying correlations among various extant landscape patterns using a layered mapping technique, a precursor to digital Geographic Information Systems (GIS). McHarg mapped each layer of a physical system, such as its topography, vegetation, and built forms, onto a transparent sheet with various tones. Each layer was drawn as a gradient from dark to light, with dark representing the greatest degree of restrictions for a particular design factor. To identify the best location for a road, for example, the topography would be toned to show the steepest areas as dark gray and the flattest areas as white, with the presumption that the flatter condition is more suitable for a road. This process would be repeated for each individual layer of the landscape, such as soil type, vegetation cover, and bodies of water. When these transparent images were superimposed, the composite map "revealed" the areas with the least amount of restrictions; that is, the areas on the map with the least amount of cumulative tones were considered best suited for a particular type of development. McHarg believed that his purportedly objective mapping procedure would guide all designers to the same outcomes and that the computer would facilitate this method. He declared that the "computer will solve the

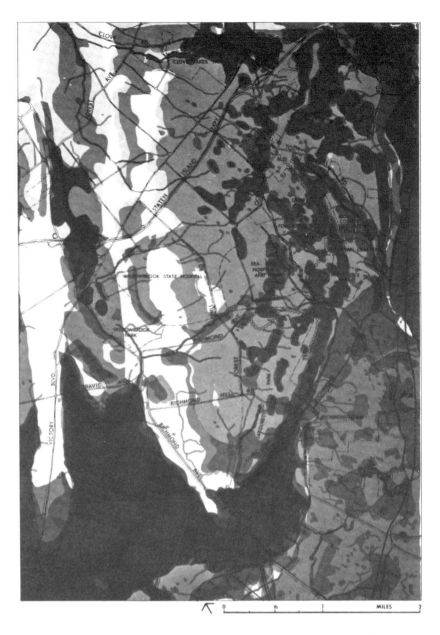

command 'show me those locations where all or most propitious factors are located, and where all or most detrimental factors are absent.'"[32]

The study of existing patterns as a means to direct new ones is sensible for obvious reasons, especially when one is determining how best to align land-use patterns with natural characteristics, as McHarg was attempting to do. Although his mapping procedure produced ample information, this information fell victim to conventional landscape imagery and forms when translated into design proposals.[33] McHarg failed to construe what an exploration of patterns might mean for experiential or spatial organization at specific sites, rather than only for land-use planning.

24. Wallace, McHarg, Roberts, and Todd, *Richmond Parkway Study*, 1968–70. Mapping of physiographic obstructions in order to determine road alignment.

> 25–26. Ian McHarg, *Delaware River Basin IV, Piedmont Upland Study*, 1969–70. Base topography map (left) and computer plot of agriculture suitability (right).

Introduction

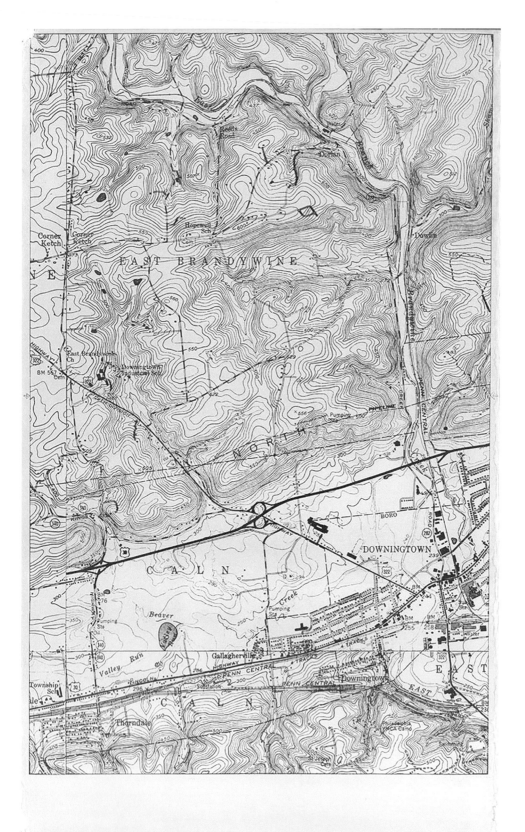

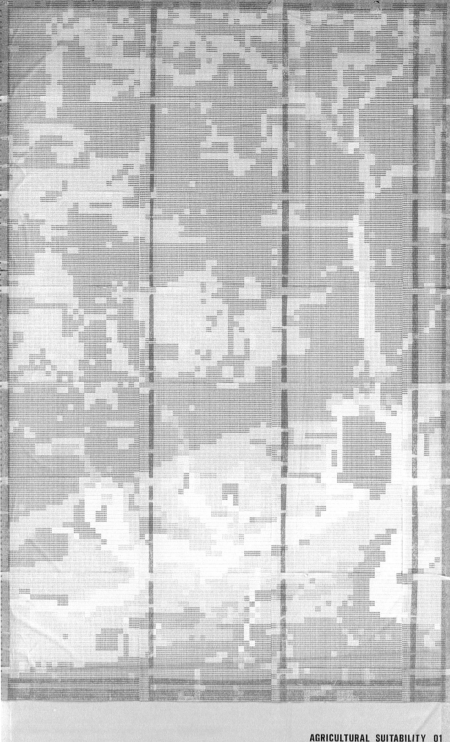

AGRICULTURAL SUITABILITY 01

PRIME

SOME LIMITATIONS

SEVERE LIMITATIONS

VERY SEVERE LIMITATIONS

NOT SUITABLE

PIEDMONT UPLAND

D.R.B. IV

In contrast to McHarg's layering method, which uses pattern-finding and analysis to determine fitness for land use, Peter Walker's layering method overlaps multiple simple geometric patterns. Eschewing a purely analytic approach, Walker turns instead to the tactics of gesture, seriality, and flatness in order to make landscape visible as "the thing itself."[34] Concerned that design has become too dependent on analysis, Walker seeks to articulate landscape's constructed nature through the deployment of visible patterns—for example, by layering planes of stone, grass, and water using a technique of formal repetition. Walker and others who promote this approach to patterning argue that it amplifies our ability to read the landscape as an intentional fabrication rather than as benign background, thereby prompting people to reflect on its significance. Critics, however, argue that geometrical patterns are autonomous and therefore unable to reflect the particulars of each site. For example, Marc Treib uses the work of Walker, alone and in collaboration with Martha Schwartz, to exemplify how patterns are limited to visual effects.[35] Treib equates pattern-making in landscape design with superficiality, maintaining that an ecological approach is "deeper," although by this term he is clearly not referring to a McHargian ecological approach.[36] Rather than using "structure, space, and pattern as content," Treib maintains that "deeper works may result from using these vehicles to embody other types of content, among them the understanding and judicious application of ecological processes."[37] In this statement, Treib suggests that patterns might be a vehicle for revealing landscape processes, but his argument generally limits a pattern to that "which begins and ends as a flat surface."[38] As this example demonstrates, the skepticism about designed surface patterns in landscape architecture derives from the belief that these patterns reflect excessive control over living matter. Uniformly ordered patterns are seen as inadequate for the task of representing our current understanding of landscapes as dynamic and fluctuating.

27. Peter Walker and Partners, *Oyama
Training Center*, Japan, 1993.

28. Peter Walker and Partners, *Hotel
Kempinski*, 1994.

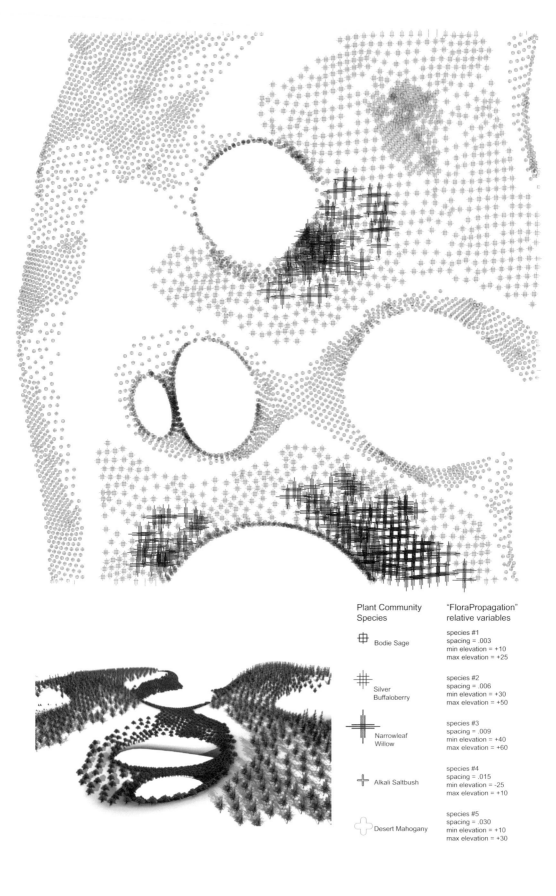

Plant Community
Species

"FloraPropagation"
relative variables

⊞ Bodie Sage

species #1
spacing = .003
min elevation = +10
max elevation = +25

╬ Silver
Buffaloberry

species #2
spacing = .006
min elevation = +30
max elevation = +50

╬ Narrowleaf
Willow

species #3
spacing = .009
min elevation = +40
max elevation = +60

✚ Alkali Saltbush

species #4
spacing = .015
min elevation = -25
max elevation = +10

✚ Desert Mahogany

species #5
spacing = .030
min elevation = +10
max elevation = +30

Patterns that Connect

As soon as people become aware that they contribute actively to their own perception, they
become much closer to the world around them.[39]
— Peter Harries-Jones

Though patterns in landscape architecture have often been
affiliated with surface geometries or superficial applications,
certain theorists have recognized their broader significance.[40]
The main purpose of Simon Bell's comprehensive treatment
in *Landscape: Pattern, Perception and Process* (1999) is to
examine the role of patterns at the scale of ecosystem management.[41] One of the primary theorizations of the association
between patterns and processes in landscapes has come
through the field of landscape ecology, which deals with flows
and movement in relation to spatial structure. Landscape
ecologists catalogue landscape patterns into spatial characteristics, such as small patches, large patches, and corridors.
They then correlate specific ecological attributes, such as
species richness, to those spatial characteristics in order to
determine how to protect key habitats and to direct development toward less ecologically significant areas.[42] Bell defends
the importance of patterns in both functional and aesthetic
terms. He argues that land management procedures must fit
the landscape's underlying structure — its given patterns — as
well as address the aesthetic dimensions of the human-made
patterns that are superimposed on that structure. Our
book also aims to find links between pattern-finding and
pattern-forming, but we do so by looking primarily at projects
that are located in urbanized areas and are not part of large-
scale managed landscapes.

More akin to our exploration is the argument made by
Anne Whiston Spirn in her article, "The Poetics of City and
Nature: Towards a New Aesthetic for Urban Design" (1988).
Spirn supports a view of ecology that celebrates aesthetic,
subjective engagement with natural processes by considering
ways in which these processes are incorporated into the

29. Chia-hua Liu, 2006. Parametric model
visualization using algorithms to explore
plant distribution and density based on
slope, aspect, and soil type.

Introduction

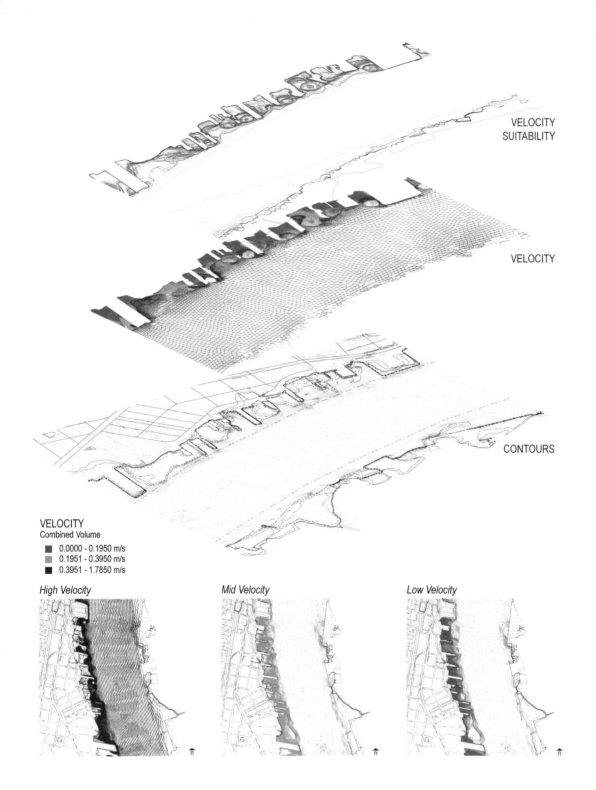

VELOCITY
SUITABILITY

VELOCITY

CONTOURS

VELOCITY
Combined Volume

■ 0.0000 - 0.1950 m/s
■ 0.1951 - 0.3950 m/s
■ 0.3951 - 1.7850 m/s

High Velocity   *Mid Velocity*   *Low Velocity*

30. PEG office of landscape +
architecture, Philadelphia, 2015.
Hydrodynamic simulation of a portion of
the Delaware River using Aquaveo SMS
and Grasshopper.

design of urban environments. Though Spirn does not address landscape pattern directly, it is an important sub-theme of her argument that she supports with images of patterns produced by radio frequencies and planetary orbits, among other sources. Spirn notes the importance of patterns formed by natural processes and suggests that they are a potential source for design: "Recent developments in mathematics and science afford new insights into the geometry and aesthetics of form generated by dynamic processes, be they natural or cultural, and point to new directions for design."[43] Furthermore, Spirn cites Gregory Bateson's notion of "patterns that connect" across time and scales, an idea of particular relevance because it overcomes the dualism of seeing patterns in terms of their environmental functions versus creating patterns for aesthetic reasons.[44] Advances in digital technology and imaging have augmented this potential significantly since Spirn's essay first appeared. With the development of parametric software, computer-controlled tools such as those used for 3D milling and printing, and access to geospatial technologies such as satellite imagery, digital elevation models, and computer fluid dynamic (CFD) models, it is possible to understand and imagine increasingly complex patterns.

Whether patterns are understood as emergent, analytical, or compositional in nature, the various approaches outlined above all share a similar ambition, which is to identify relationships between natural and cultural domains. Patterns are vehicles for rendering processes comprehensible; form, composition, and repetition are means by which what is fluid and changing becomes perceptible. As Spirn notes, recurrences are necessary because without them "time would be an imperceptible, formless flow."[45] Likewise, Bateson scholar Peter Harries-Jones states that it is difficult to understand change without a point of reference; understanding "requires some form of sense or instrument which will indicate patterns of *both* change *and* not-change."[46]

Accordingly, we focus in this book on techniques that utilize formal or temporal recurrences in order to convey environmental recurrences. In doing so, we respond to Bateson's assertion that it is "of prime importance to have a conceptual system which will force us to see the 'message' (e.g. the art object) as *both* itself internally patterned *and* itself a part of a larger patterned universe."[47] Addressing both ends of the spectrum—the perceptual and the material—is critical to developing an ecological consciousness capable of overcoming the dualisms that have often plagued discussions in landscape architecture since the discipline's adoption of the ecological mandate. As architectural historian Christopher Hight so eloquently states:

> [The] aesthetic is interwoven into the history of discourses of the environment and the production of ecological concepts, such that an ecological design ethic is not detachable from its formal, graphic, and spatial concepts. This does not produce harmony between Nature and Culture, but brings the inhuman into the realm of our senses and sensation, and constructs alternative assemblages between processes and forms.[48]

As the ideas and projects presented in the following chapters demonstrate, patterns are one way to consider such alternative assemblages. Patterns can link the ecological and infrastructural mandates placed on landscapes without forsaking formal and perceptual coherence. This approach follows in the footsteps of Bateson's ecological episteme, which is rooted in recursive communication that attempts to link the natural and cultural realms.[49]

31. Mark Nystrom, *Wind Process 2012.01.*

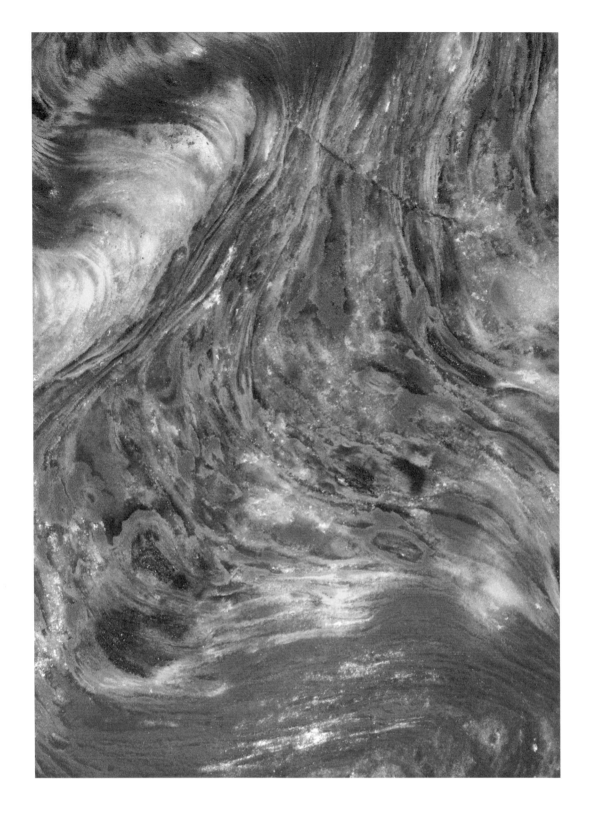

1. Photomicrography of fossilized
stromatolite.

2. Satellite radar image of Keraf Suture,
Sudan, 2009.
Buried beneath layers of sand, this
Precambrian geologic feature was
recently unearthed through new imaging
technology.

A topological description of a pattern is concerned not with exact values of distances and angles but rather with the number of connections.[1]
—A. L. Loeb

The pervasiveness of data and sensing technologies has led to an increased ability to visualize the physical processes that give rise to identifiable patterns in landscapes. Both visible and invisible characteristics are catalogued and translated into pixels, points, and lines so that the description of a terrain is no longer limited to mapping its spatial structure or perceptible features alone; rather, the description also represents its *topological* properties, which chart relationships among a variety of processes that flow through the landscape.[2] This chapter delineates two kinds of topological patterns: *divisible* and *accretive*. Although the two are not mutually exclusive, divisible patterns define the spatial structure of a surface, such as its topography, whereas accretive patterns simulate processes upon or near that surface, such as water flow. In computational models, both divisible and accretive patterns are shaped as much by data as by the direct manipulation of geometries. That is, many of the patterns described in this chapter are indirectly structured and numerically *informed* as much as they are directly drawn. They are generated by algorithms in which one or more constraints, such as slope or distance, govern their entire shape and organization. Consequently, patterns are imbued with quantitative information in ways that were not previously possible. As both "datascapes" and landscapes, these patterns are inseparable from the virtual and physical milieus from which they arise.[3]

Typology (Things) and Topology (Relations)

The study and creation of patterns involves the transfer of organized information from one medium to another.[4] This transfer is aided by procedure-based computer modeling, which facilitates recursive design methods. Recursion is embedded in both computational techniques, where sequences of operations are

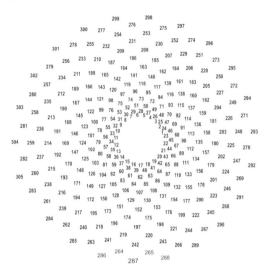

Index Numbers

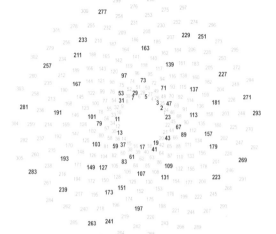

Prime Numbers

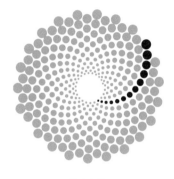

Modulo 13

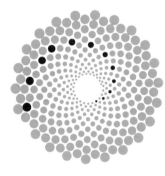

Modulo 21

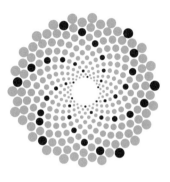

Modulo 6

3. Joshua Freese and Jieping Wang, 2016.
Various spiral patterns traced through
different step functions. In each sample,
the structure of the model remains
constant.

4. Spiral pattern of sunflower.

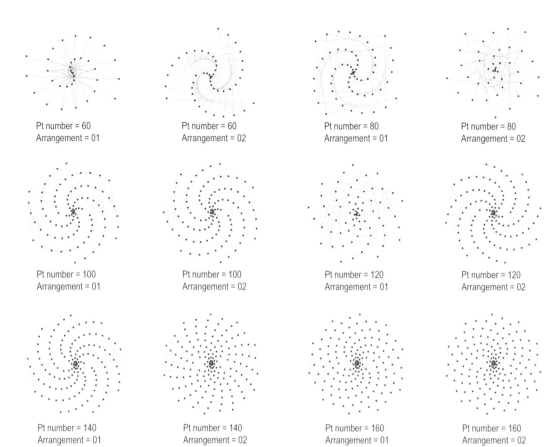

Pt number = 60
Arrangement = 01

Pt number = 60
Arrangement = 02

Pt number = 80
Arrangement = 01

Pt number = 80
Arrangement = 02

Pt number = 100
Arrangement = 01

Pt number = 100
Arrangement = 02

Pt number = 120
Arrangement = 01

Pt number = 120
Arrangement = 02

Pt number = 140
Arrangement = 01

Pt number = 140
Arrangement = 02

Pt number = 160
Arrangement = 01

Pt number = 160
Arrangement = 02

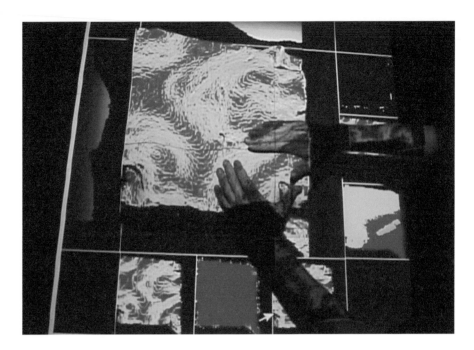

used as feedback loops, and the resultant forms, i.e., patterns. Recursion provided the foundation of Gregory Bateson's ecological epistemology; he believed that, since the development of the universe and of life is recursive, our methods and models should also be recursive so that they will best reflect how communication happens. In the natural world, for example, form is a process of differentiation that occurs incrementally during an organism's development instead of being established from the outset.[5] Differentiation takes place through the relationships among the various parts in conjunction with the external environmental forces that affect these relationships. Although the various stages of development share common characteristics, the differences among them are most significant, since they produce diversity of form. Thus, form is an embodiment of difference. As architect Stan Allen summarizes, "Differences of configuration, pattern, or shape make sense only when put into play within a larger field of differences. Change is redefined as difference over time, and all form becomes relational, based on interval and change."[6]

Using morphogenetic processes in nature as an inspiration for thinking about computational techniques in design, patterns can be understood as relational and dynamic ways of organizing rather than static ones.[7] As Bateson explains:

5. MIT Media Lab, *Illuminating Clay*, 2004. This technology uses open-source geospatial information to generate real-time analysis of changes made to a terrain. These models combine the physical media of clay with computational imagery. Physical changes made to the clay are captured, analyzed, and projected back to the model's surface.

> We have been trained to think of patterns, with the exception of those of music, as fixed affairs. It is easier and lazier that way but, of course, all nonsense. In truth, the right way to begin to think about the pattern which connects is to think of it as *primarily* ... a dance of interacting parts and

only secondarily pegged down by various sorts of physical limits.[8]

Computational models should have particular relevance for landscape architecture, given the temporal and relational qualities inherent in the landscape medium. Even though much has been written about the importance of determining better ways to engage such qualities, there has been little change in the analytical or representational techniques that should accompany such a shift. The media used for design have changed profoundly in the last fifteen years, yet few landscape architects have taken up the challenge of investigating the potentials and limitations associated with such changes. Apart from spatial analytics and GIS, digital media used in landscape architecture have remained largely within the realm of two-dimensional explorations that replicate manual drawing techniques, such as mapping and montage.[9] Even vector-based GIS software utilizes pre-classified, two-dimensional geometric entities. This overreliance on two-dimensional geometry and raster-based image making reinforces typological thinking because the supporting design methods are based on simple classifications, such as layering previously established shape files or images. The intention behind, and the consequence of, classification is often replication. This results in the reproduction of recognizable landscape types, such as wetlands, and the uncritical transfer of elements from one place to another without significant alteration or correlation with their specific circumstances. The implicit assumption is that, if a landscape is drawn to look similar to a type, it will behave accordingly. This limits pattern to its common association as "a form or model proposed for imitation."[10] In contrast, understanding patterns topologically, through three-dimensional computational models, liberates them from this restricted definition.
  Topology is the mathematical study of shapes and spaces that retain properties of connectedness while undergoing continuous deformation, such as curving and bending. Topological patterns, therefore, comprise an ordered array of such shapes and spaces in which all entities combine to create

                  Dynamic Patterns: Visualizing Landscapes in a Digital Age

6. A. L. Loeb, 1971. The top pair of drawings shows topologically equivalent patterns. The only difference is that one is symmetrical (left) and the other is deformed.

7. A. L. Loeb, 1971. The bottom pair of drawings shows topologically different patterns. In the left drawing, each segment (thick black line) has three points of connection at one end (itself and two neighbors), whereas in the right drawing each segment has four points of connection at one end. Also, the shapes that compose the pattern in the drawing on the left share six neighboring shapes, while the pattern on the right has only four.

a network. The etymology of topology derives from the Greek *topos,* "place," and *logos,* "speaking, discourse, treatise, doctrine, theory, science."[11] In Latin, the term was *analysis situs,* which emphasizes the study of a situation.[12] In the late nineteenth to early twentieth century, topology became identified within a branch of mathematics as the study of *continuity.*[13] In contrast to Euclidean geometry, topology describes relationships among entities that remain unaltered through change. Topological surfaces are formed by interconnected points and vectors rather than by discrete coordinates, and by calculus and differential geometry (the study of change) rather than by fixed geometric shapes (the study of constants). In topology, metrics like length or area are not stable, yet the connectivity among elements is preserved. For instance, the points in a bent lattice will have different locations and distances between them (variances) yet retain an equal degree of connection (invariance).[14] Given that landscape design involves the manipulation of interrelated surfaces and materials that are bound to physical localities yet open to environmental influences, topology is an apt framework for thinking about and working with landscapes.[15]

Facilitated by computational modeling, topological thinking in design has expanded the means by which to engage in interactions with both fixed and changing entities. All changes in topological space are intensive, rather than discrete, because modifications made to any one entity have a reciprocal effect on neighboring entities. Because they are not restricted to quantitative analysis, such tools can open up the imagination by offering a relational and time-dependent means for working with landscape. For example, parametric models enable information such as force, quantity, and direction of wind or water

8. Marine stratocumulus clouds frequently form parallel rows, or "cloud streets," along the direction of wind flow. When the flow is interrupted by an obstacle such as an island, a series of organized eddies can appear within the cloud layer downwind of the obstacle.

9. Leonardo da Vinci, *A Deluge,* c. 1517–18, black chalk on paper, 15.9cm x 20.3cm.

> 10. These multi-colored geological formations, located in China's Gansu Province, are the result of layers of sandstone, limestone, and minerals deposited during the Jurassic and Tertiary periods.

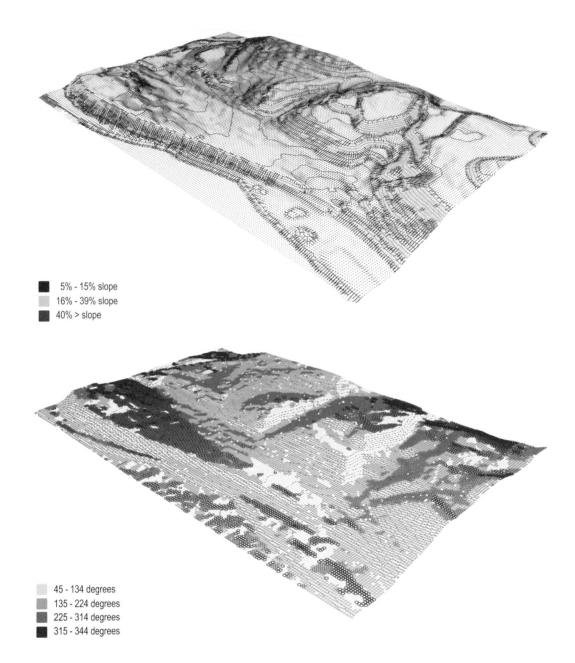

5% - 15% slope
16% - 39% slope
40% > slope

45 - 134 degrees
135 - 224 degrees
225 - 314 degrees
315 - 344 degrees

11. PEG office of landscape +
architecture, 2015. Parametric software
(Grasshopper) is used for terrain
analysis. Slope is shown as colored
hachure lines (top) and aspect is shown
as colored circles (bottom).

flow to be expressed as related datasets. Changing the flow alters the profile, and vice versa. The association between information and formation is therefore inherent in the model, enabling it to incorporate both continuity and difference as complementary properties. The presence of differences—local deviations in intensity—elicits change. For that reason, patterns should be understood, not as inert entities, but as events—as the "meeting-points of actions," to use György Kepes's phrase.[16] As a generative design tool, this type of modeling fosters a shift from "thing-seeing" to pattern-seeing.[17] Although the tools for making this shift are relatively new, the agenda is not. The tools have simply provided more integrated ways to cultivate recursive design methods that can engage the complexity and mutability of the "dance of interacting parts" that characterizes landscapes.

Structuring Patterns

> In order to design for movement, a whole new system of conceptualizing must be undertaken. Our present systems of design and planning are inevitably limited by our techniques of conceptualizing and our methods of symbolizing ideas. We know only how to delineate static objects, and so that is all that we do.[18]
> —Lawrence Halprin

> On the largest and smallest scale, we find serial elements, repetitive patterns. … And if we turn our eyes to the great natural domains, periodicity expands to include the ocean itself.[19]
> —Hans Jenny

Lawrence Halprin's work with notational drawings and Kepes and Hans Jenny's experiments with sound and vibration illustrate clearly how patterns are a consequence of interactions.

Halprin developed a methodology with his wife Anna, a dancer, which he published in 1969 in his book *The RSVP*

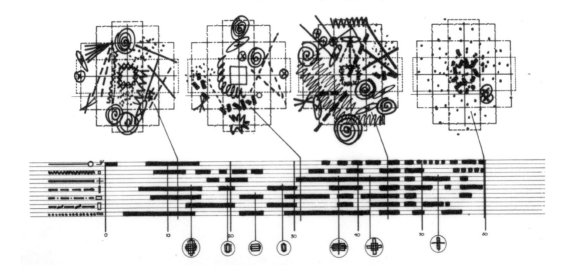

12. Lawrence Halprin, *Overhoff-Halprin fountain*, 1962 World's Fair, Seattle. The score choreographs various water effects produced by water pressure and quantity, wind, nozzle configuration, and timing of water sprays.

13. *Overhoff-Halprin fountain*, photograph.

Cycles: Creative Processes in the Human Environment.[20] With this methodology, he endorsed a proto-computational approach to landscape design, maintaining that time and movement, which are the invisible aspects of a work, are best engaged through notational diagrams that celebrate patterns of process and performance. The techniques developed by the Halprins drew directly from performance art and cybernetics, two fields in which notation figures prominently. Stan Allen outlines several key characteristics of notations, the most relevant to this discussion being that they engage "invisibles" by specifying relationships rather than objects, include time as a variable, and work through differences rather than resemblances.[21] This last point is relevant to the aforementioned description of topology, where the emphasis is on intensive difference and pattern rather than on pictorial image and type. The notational language of *The RSVP Cycles* engages all of these aspects, and it became Halprin's means of advancing his notion of performativity in design. The RSVP method, which employed what he called "scores," entailed the use of analog algorithmic processes. Scores comprise diagrams and tables that produce a matrix of relations, and they function as a tool for directing someone to carry out an activity based on a set of instructions. The scores are not meant to produce predefined ends but to initiate a course of action, and they are continually refined throughout the decision-making process of a cycle.[22] As landscape historian Margot Lystra notes, the scores "operated as immersions into open systems. They evoked shifting and unpredictable soundscapes and landscapes whose surprises were understood, not as problems, but as sources of aesthetic inspiration and delight."[23] The scores, though open, were not random or arbitrary. Rather, they evolved through very explicit procedures orchestrated by the designer.[24]

The inclusion of metrical, numerical, and textual data in the scores transformed common graphic descriptions into notational instructions for realizing new arrangements in time and space. Instead of describing a specific object through the immediacy of pictorial imagery or the conventions of orthographic drawing, the scores specified movement patterns among different elements or agents, which were invoked through the abstraction of alphanumeric figures. They served as a method to uncover and produce conditions that could not be imagined using standard drawing techniques. Lystra, writing about the representational differences between McHarg's and Halprin's interpretations of cybernetics, observes that "it is through drawing practices that designers enact specific relationships between themselves and the landscapes they draw. Accordingly, drawing methods determine the very nature of [the] relationship between designer and landscape [which,] in turn, alters the characters, qualities, and capacities of the landscape that is depicted, designed, and constructed."[25]

Although the thinking that formed the basis of *The RSVP Cycles* enabled Halprin to achieve some remarkable projects, the advantage of such notational methods can also be a limitation, since the drawings lack specific links to the dimensions of a surface or form. Although the design process is

recursive, the diagrams themselves do not necessarily produce the subsequent form of a project. Nevertheless, the algorithmic method produces results through the orchestration of a sequence of events in time, thereby acting as an analog to the generative rules of computational models.

Kepes's experiments with fire and sound and Hans Jenny's work with sand and sound are particularly salient from the perspective of computation in relation to physical processes. Kepes and Jenny both explored wave phenomena by looking at the relationship between acoustics and pattern. Their work demonstrates the role of forces in shaping matter into dynamic but ordered formations, using vibration to produce a form of patterning that is continuous yet differentiated from its milieu. Rather than stable figures that resist external influence, these patterns are characterized by a high degree of flux arising from slight modifications of the relationships among very few elements. For example, Kepes's *Flame Orchard* (1971), created in collaboration with another artist, a physicist, and a composer, incorporated a metal container with a hollow cavity within which gas was introduced.[26] Holes drilled in the container's top allowed gas to rise above its surface and become ignited, and variations in the shapes of the flames were produced by varying the sound within the chamber via a speaker. Similarly, Jenny investigated the relationship between patterns and frequency by covering metal plates with sand and then introducing vibration to the plates. This produced very distinct patterns that transitioned from one fungible figure into another. Each pattern gave rise to new patterns. As Jenny stated, "At one moment a pattern is closed and separate; at another the same element is open and linked up with its environment."[27] This form of dynamic patterning is conditional upon motion, stable at some times and open at others.

Analogously to Halprin's scores, the processes by which Kepes and Jenny produced patterns involved the orchestration of a sequence of events in time. These processes act as analogs to the generative rules of procedure-based computer models. The experiments demonstrate that patterning is a general property of complex systems, forming orderly arrays

14. György Kepes, *Flame Orchard*, 1972, sound-animated gas flames.

Dynamic Patterns: Visualizing Landscapes in a Digital Age

15. Hans Jenny, 1967, steel plate and sand.
The sporadic figures are a product of changes in the environment, which are produced through the presence of vibration at different frequencies. All states of formation and transformation in the patterns are indications of the feedback among its constituent elements: material (sand grain size), force (wave length produced by varying frequency), and field (the plate shape and size upon which the sand is placed).

16. Étienne-Jules Marey. *Study: High Jump*, 1886, chronophotograph.

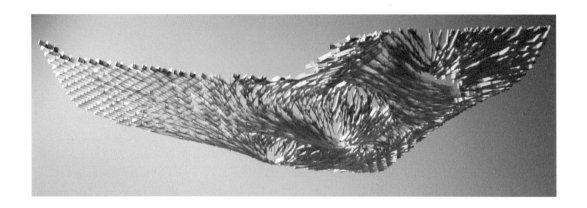

17. **PEG office of landscape + architecture, 2012.**
Hachures became outmoded with the invention of contours; however, contemporary surface descriptions using hachures are reemerging today through digital media. Unlike the contour, hachure drawings express the qualitative impression of a terrain. This physical model represents both water quantity (by length) and quality (by thickness).

based on simple rules and local interactions. Similarly, the structures that underlie digital media are repetitive processes laden with patterns—procedural repetitions such as copy, array, and scale. Points, lines, and surfaces are rudimentarily defined and then progressively altered by adjusting their values and variables. Through a process of iteration and recursion, computational modeling enables the creation of highly complex topological patterns that are designed in response to multiple and overlapping organizational, environmental, and experiential criteria. Accordingly, the ways in which information and forma-tion relate to each other are comparable in topological and natural patterns.[28]

Divisible Patterns

> [M]any natural patterns result from mathematical analogies and equivalences in the rules governing their formation.[29]
> —Philip Ball

As discussed in the introductory chapter, conspicuous pattern-ing in landscape architecture has often been characterized as antithetical to process, though closer examination indicates that patterning is in fact a form of information that is both guided by and expressive of processes. With this definition in mind, the projects described below are characterized by two types of morphology—*divisible* and *accretive*—that are distinguished by how patterns are used to analyze and struc-ture relationships.

Divisible patterns are typically composed of a network of polygons that define topological surfaces, such as those found in the land. These networks are created by the continuous joining of one or more geometric shapes, such as rectangles, triangles, and hexagons, resulting in such tessellated struc-tures as meshes, triangulated irregular networks (TINs), or Voronoi diagrams. These tessellations are commonly used in digital terrain modeling and have been widely explored as a way to generate site organizations based on data points.

18. Jing Guo, 2014. Computer-generated
flow model, laser-etched on stacked
sheets of acrylic.

19. Freeland Buck, *Spiral Tessellation*, 2011.

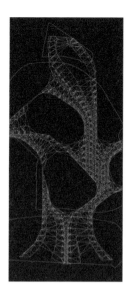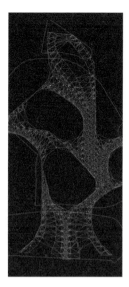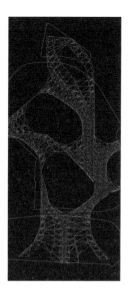

20. Edwin Lam and Sean Stevenson, *Prophylactic Landscape*, 2011.
A series of drawings exploring different water flow volumes across a faceted ground surface. The red areas represent low points where the greatest volume of water would collect.

Computational models do not have to be patterned in their structure if they are not created through an orderly array of shapes; however, using an orderly array of points or shapes to create topological surfaces means that the surfaces are composed of networks, which are inherently relational. In this way, surfaces are formed by first choosing at least three points of geospatial data (e.g., spot elevations) drawn from field surveys or remote surveying methods. This information is then used to define the network boundary, polygon shape, and resolution (i.e., the size and density of the polygon).

In contrast to scaled drawings, which are uniform across the full area covered (for instance through the use of regular increments of contour lines on a map), computational models do not have a fixed scale or hierarchy of information.[30] Rather, these models can incorporate multiple scales of information simultaneously while remaining continuous. Thus, for example, after the initial network resolution is set to the appropriate scale of study, it can be further subdivided in order to alter parts of the network selectively and thereby provide more or less detail about its surface. Given that networks are systemic because their entities are interconnected, patterns can be refined iteratively and incrementally in response to a host of specific design objectives and site contingencies, including slope, drainage, or sun angle. Because landscapes can simultaneously exhibit high levels of diversity and of spatial and material continuity, the introduction of more nuanced criteria enables the production of higher levels of "fitness" in the analysis and creation of patterns. GIS layers, by contrast, are all of the same scale and therefore do not vary with respect to the "content" of different kinds of information. A computational model can also be distinguished from a collage, which is multi-scalar and multi-informational yet discontinuous in its structure.

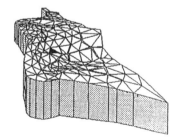

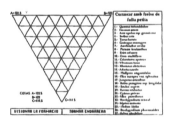

21. Carlos Ferrater, Bet Figueras, and
José Luís Canosa, *Barcelona Botanical
Garden*, 2007.

22. *Barcelona Botanical Garden*.

23. TIN of the *Barcelona Botanical Garden*
site.

Two recent projects that exhibit the potential of topological patterns to adapt to a range of scales and conditions
are the 2007 *Barcelona Botanical Garden* by Carlos Ferrater and
Bet Figueras and Plasma Studio/Ground Lab's *Flowing Gardens*
master plan for the 2011 Xi'an International Horticultural Expo.
Although both projects occupy former industrial sites in dense
urban areas and both use TINs, they differ in the manner in
which the designers deploy patterning to exploit and accentu-
ate their respective sites and programs. Whereas the *Barcelona
Botanical Garden* is located on a steep hillside, *Flowing Gardens*
is on a gradually sloping site adjoining Guangyun Lake. The
design of the Barcelona garden is intensely sectional, accentuating the extant topography, and is multi-directional in structure
on the macro scale of the site; the *Flowing Gardens*, by contrast,
emphasizes a central, directed movement through the site from
the entrance to the lake. The botanical garden uses the faceted network (TIN) to structure elements that simultaneously
complement and contrast with the steeply sloped site, while
the organizing geometry of *Flowing Gardens* zigzags across the
site following the contours of the existing topography, which
produces more uniform gradients of elevation change, a quality
suggested by the project's name. The experiential difference
between the two projects seems to be one of moving *in* the terrain in Barcelona but moving *on* it and *with* it in Xi'an.
Plasma Studio/Ground Lab's use of divisible patterning for both site and building organization deftly blends
architecture and landscape within a seamless geometric continuum. Geometric repetition produces a clear and coherent
spatial identity while accommodating the diversity of pavilion
styles inherent in exposition programs. This approach clearly
demonstrates how patterning can be used to challenge and

24. Plasma Studio and Ground Lab, *Xi'an
International Horticultural Expo*, 2011.

Topological Patterns

destabilize such normative disciplinary categories as architecture and landscape architecture. Its efficacy does not, however, assert the same transformative potency in the landscape itself, either spatially or materially. The planting, for instance, consists primarily of large planar figures filled with monocultures. This arrangement perhaps reaffirms Marc Treib's criticism of how patterning has been employed in designed landscapes. Introducing variety in both the composition and plant species, based on aspect or slope, for instance, could have further invigorated the pattern by creating a broader array of effects and forms of horticultural display, such as the temporal patterns of bloom periods or differing growth rates. Nevertheless, *Flowing Gardens* persuasively depicts the formal and functional adaptability of topological patterns.

The design of the *Barcelona Botanical Garden* reflects the pliable nature of topological patterns that locally adapt and diversify based on formal and functional needs without compromising the identity of the system as a whole; the project thus has aesthetic coherence without being homogenous. The topological patterns of the digital model heighten the topographic engagement with the ground. Ferrater and Figueras created a series of alterations among crowns, crevices, and coplanar surfaces that selectively follow or diverge from the extant contours. Through this forming process, they refined and evaluated the TIN network iteratively to minimize earth-moving expenses and to balance cut and fill soil volumes. They honed the pattern further based on the slope and solar aspects of the selected plant communities in order to mimic the growing conditions of the plants' native habitats.[31] Ferrater and Figueras subsequently adapted their design to incorporate the irrigation demands and drainage of these planted microclimates, moving from drier uplands to wetter lowlands. The visitor's movement is guided on paths that follow the faceted network across and against the slope of the hillside, which provides either cuts for seating niches or projections for raised outlooks. In this sense, faceting is performative in both utilitarian and aesthetic ways, transcending merely functional requirements and becoming inextricably embedded in both the form and experience of the garden in relation to its situation. As this example shows, the recursive layering of information can produce a pattern that feels derived from rather than applied to its site.

Accretive Patterns

> Magnitude and direction are interrelated; together, they set the stage for the emergence of something new. A sufficient increase or decrease in magnitude brings a pattern to its limit, to the line of demarcation which closes it and opens up another pattern.[32]
> —György Kepes

Accretive patterns offer a way to visualize environmental factors that elude such conventional surface descriptions as the use of contour lines to describe topography. They are used to simulate behaviors within atmospheres or surfaces, such as air or hydrological flows. Because accretive patterns are typically constituted by aggregations of points or lines, they are well suited to depict aspects of the landscape or environment that involve gradients, tones, or transitions arising from such forces as direction, intensity, and duration. In contrast to networks of divisible patterns, these forces are not easily represented by shape because they describe movements, transformations, and actions, and are thus better represented by fields of intensity that then guide or inform how shapes are inscribed within these fields. In other words, the geometric structure of a surface is not defined at the outset, as it is in selecting a divisible pattern based on a TIN or Voronoi diagram. Instead, the selection of a geometric structure is predicated upon what is considered the most appropriate organization for augmenting flows, and on the qualities that its connections and directions would enable. For example, a branching structure would lead to very different outcomes than a spiral structure. Furthermore, because accretive patterns deal with movement and change, they can be mapped over different time frames, thereby revealing other patterns through comparative analysis, such as how concentrations

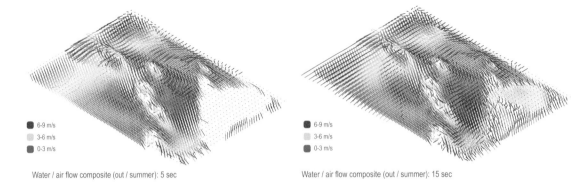

6-9 m/s
3-6 m/s
0-3 m/s

Water / air flow composite (out / summer): 5 sec

6-9 m/s
3-6 m/s
0-3 m/s

Water / air flow composite (out / summer): 15 sec

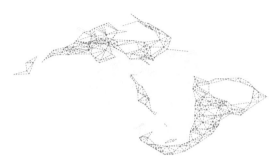

High turbulence intensity field (out / summer): 5 sec

High turbulence intensity field (out / summer): 15 sec

25. PEG office of landscape +
architecture, Biscayne Bay, Miami,
2012. Water and air flow composite
simulations (top row). Tessellated
areas show zones of highest turbulence
(bottom row).

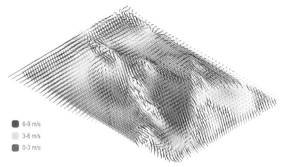

6-9 m/s
3-6 m/s
0-3 m/s

Water / air flow composite (out / summer): 25 sec

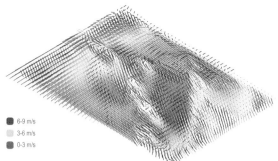

6-9 m/s
3-6 m/s
0-3 m/s

Water / air flow composite (out / summer): 35 sec

High turbulence intensity field (out / summer): 25 sec

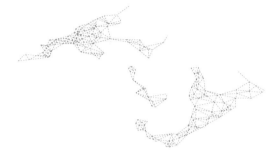

High turbulence intensity field (out / summer): 35 sec

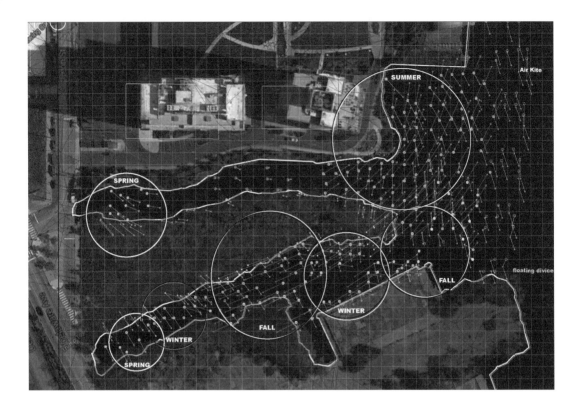

Labels within image: SUMMER, Air Kite, SPRING, floating divice, FALL, WINTER, FALL, WINTER, SPRING

26–27. Elise McCurley, Leeju Kang, Chris Arth, *Gliding Networks*, Philadelphia, 2014.
A series of kites anchored in the water register changing air and water patterns in the Delaware River.

of air particulates differ based on seasonal wind direction and temperature.

A high degree of feedback between pattern-finding and pattern-forming occurs when one works with accretive patterns. Modeling various states requires the selection of one or more parameters that simulate real-world behaviors or attributes. In *Edaphic Effects*, for example, we (PEG office of landscape + architecture) used a series of hydrodynamic simulations to study the implications of water flow across a site. The purpose of this project was to design an area for storm-water infiltration using customized geo-cells, which are at- or sub-grade three-dimensional structures used for water infiltration and soil stabilization. Beginning with the existing topography and estimated rainfall quantities, a series of parametric models was used to visualize different runoff and collection patterns by adjusting slope-to-depth ratios to guide and collect water. These visualizations were in turn used to test various configurations that simultaneously related the overall form of the topography to the distribution of the geo-cells that composed its surface. More specifically, changes in the profile of the topography affected the flow pattern, which in turn altered the density and size of the geo-cells and the ratio of grass to gravel infill. The variation expressed on the surface conveys the processes that underlie it.

A similar approach to generating organization based on modeling environmental factors can be seen in Catherine Mosbach and Philippe Rahm's *Phase Shifts Park* in Taichung,

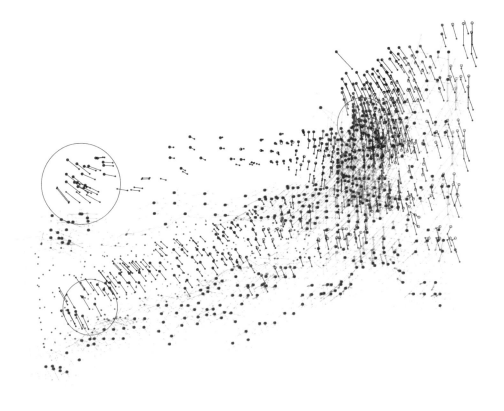

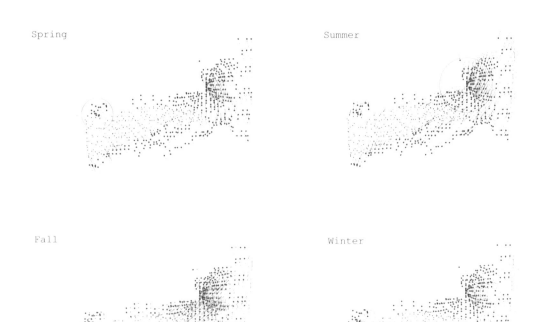

Spring

Summer

Fall

Winter

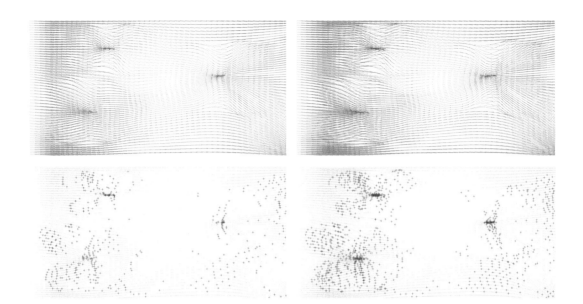

28. **PEG** office of landscape + architecture, *Edaphic Effects*, Philadelphia, 2011.
Simulations testing water flow as a product of slope and water quantity (top row). The plusses show points of flow convergence (bottom row). Their quantity and distribution were used to determine geo-cell size.

Taiwan. Their analysis of unseen influences, such as humidity, wind, and pollution, provided the basis for the subsequent development of the park's overall structure as well as for individual elements and fixtures within it. Their intent was to take advantage of and intensify the distinction between higher, drier, breezier areas and lower, wetter, more stagnant ones. Using meteorological data and computational fluid dynamic simulations, they located the coldest, driest, and cleanest areas of the site, represented through a series of flow and gradient patterns. They then used these patterns to devise topographic, planting, and mechanical means of altering the extant climatic patterns into distinct microclimates. For example, they used a heat map, based on the northeast wind that delivers cooler air, to determine the locations where they would place heat-reducing devices such as atomizers and dehumidifiers. The areas least affected by the breezes were selected for the placement of water collection basins in order to make these areas more humid, thereby increasing the contrast between highlands and lowlands. In this example, perceptible patterns are not locatable in geometry or form *per se* but result from the increased contrast among temperature and humidity zones. Subtly changing environmental shifts of pollution levels, humidity, and heat are rendered more palpable through the repetition, location, and groupings of follies. Through such technological extensions, these differences can be sensed as thresholds.

The two approaches to modeling outlined here—divisible and accretive—do not exclude geospatial analysis. In *Edaphic Effects*, for example, we used GIS to prioritize site selection at the urban scale and then coupled this information with the flow visualizations at the site scale. This approach is similar to the nested scales of information that Nicholas de Monchaux used in *Local Code: Real Estates,* in which he applied GIS mapping for initial site selection and parametric tools to

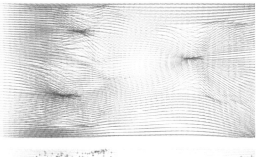

29. *Edaphic Effects*. Geo-cell pattern on surface of infiltration area.

produce site-specific variations. Using databases from GIS, Google, and other web-based sources, de Monchaux selected 525 parcels from the city of San Francisco's stock of vacant land based on their potential to capture stormwater and reduce the heat-island effect. After site selection, he analyzed the characteristics of each site, including wind speed, hydrology, and existing vegetation, using place-based environmental models. The information derived from this analysis was then parametrically modeled to determine the location and relative proportion of paths, trees, and landforms desired to augment the environmental performance of each site. The project's overall aim was to construct a network of "reparative" interventions out of small, discontinuous sites that, in aggregate, could create larger environmental benefits.[33]

Although de Monchaux states that *Local Code* would provide a framework for use by community stakeholders, the model incorporates only quantifiable criteria. This problem-solving approach could result in the codification of a kit-of-parts, resulting in homogeneity among sites rather than opening up opportunities by running multiple scenarios, in a process that would be more akin to Halprin's search for aesthetic inspiration. The risk is that the method could become aligned with McHarg's narrow belief that, with one model and the punch of a button, the computer could account for all design variables. Still, the approach used in *Local Code* is useful for diversifying approaches to current vacant land programs, which typically impose a single design solution on all sites. *Local Code* is conceived of as a network of regional "green infrastructure" that is differentiated at a local scale. As such, the project exhibits the potential to combine geospatial and parametric tools, thereby linking the processes of pattern-finding and pattern-forming by bridging scales that are too often addressed independently.

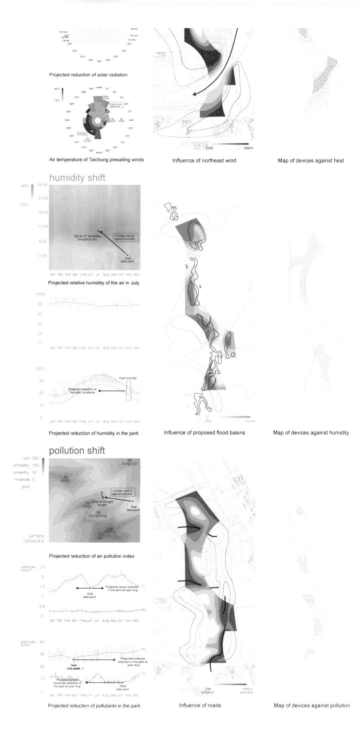

Projected reduction of solar radiation

Air temperature of Taichung prevailing winds

Influence of northeast wind

Map of devices against heat

humidity shift

Projected relative humidity of the air in July

Projected reduction of humidity in the park

Influence of proposed flood basins

Map of devices against humidity

pollution shift

Projected reduction of air pollution index

Projected reduction of pollutants in the park

Influence of roads

Map of devices against pollution

30. Philippe Rahm and Catherine Mosbach, *Phase Shifts Park*, Taichung, Taiwan, 2012–15.
Computational fluid dynamic (CFD) simulations were used to map the distribution and concentration of pollution, heat, and humidity in the existing site. These simulations were used to establish a spatial framework of microclimatic gradients.

31. *Phase Shifts Park*. Microclimate zones and topography derived from CFD simulations.

Conclusion: From Things to Patterns

> Leading us away from the system of fixed *things*, and toward the system of spatio-temporal patterns, the newly revealed visible world brings us to the threshold of a new vision.[34]
> —György Kepes

The topological patterns highlighted in this chapter point the way toward design methods that link process and organization, information and formation. Patterns are the transfer of organized information from one medium to another, including information that is not immediately detectable. They are the "surface" expression of underlying interactions and movements. Patterns are both physical and representational; they contain both organization and "image." They belong to a particular place because they are derived from localized information, yet they are also distinct from their milieu owing to their legibility.

The repetition inherent in patterns refers not only to the feedback processes intrinsic to natural or computational systems but also to experience. As Peter Harries-Jones argues, "If all is flux, and everything is changing and nothing remains the same, then it is difficult for the observers, who are also changing, to construct any point of reference."[35] Patterns can be recognized by comparing repetitive events occurring over time so as to gain an awareness of *change* versus *lack of change*. Spans of time or space between occurrences—temporal gaps—are central to the notion of behavioral patterns, which is the topic of the next chapter. As with topological patterns, the modes of visualization employed are intended to facilitate the recognition of difference—a shift from seeing things to seeing patterns in the dance among interacting parts.

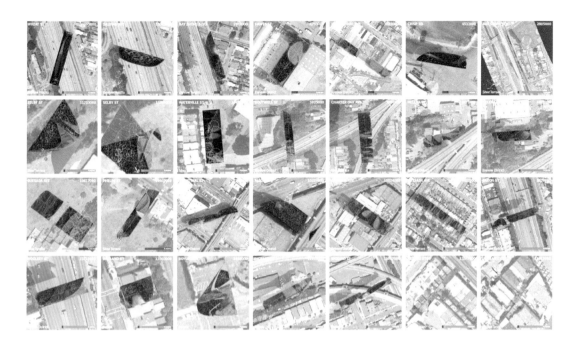

32. Nicholas de Monchaux, *Local Code:
Real Estates*, San Francisco, 2011.
Sampling of vacant sites with proposed
transformations.

Behavioral Patterns

1. György Kepes, *Fluid Forms*, 1944, high
speed photograph, 10" x 8".

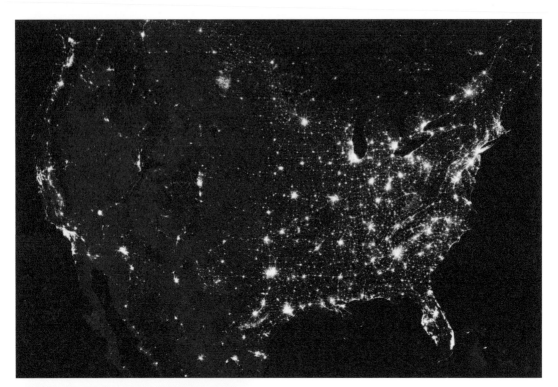

2. Satellite image of artificial light
across the continental United States.
The Visible Infrared Imaging Radiometer
Suite (VIIRS) optical system enables
the detection of dim signals at night
by isolating the green to near-infrared
wavelengths.

3. Claudia Mitchell is the first person
to receive a mind-controlled bionic arm
(2006).

Behavioral patterns are relevant for thinking about relationships among entities separated in time and space. Though some of the topological patterns in the previous chapter describe behaviors, those examples were confined to the organization of bounded sites and contiguous terrain. By contrast, the behavioral patterns depicted in this chapter do not have an identifiable location.[1] This makes them especially pertinent for describing phenomena whose boundaries are mutable and where distinctions among "individual" entities are physically or conceptually unsettled. For example, on a macro scale, environmental patterns such as those pertaining to ozone depletion or global warming are not directly experienced owing to their remote, intangible, and dispersive nature; similarly, on a micro scale, the genetic engineering of crops, drugs, and animals has made the distinction between technology and biology increasingly difficult to maintain. Categorizations such as nature–culture, body–environment, and human–nonhuman are no longer tenable for both philosophical and material reasons. As a result, the conceptual framework of system and environment has replaced the categorical division of nature and culture.[2] Because patterns are relational, they are conducive to this reformulation; patterns perform systemically rather than categorically. Behavioral patterns, in particular, bridge scales by linking the behavior of physical systems or beings, such as energy or animals, to abstract systems, such as information expressed as digital signs. In other words, behavioral patterns are made visible through information and communication technologies that mediate between material processes and our perception of these processes.

The contemporary projects in this chapter share a conceptual lineage with mid-twentieth-century art practices, specifically those influenced by systems thinking and cybernetics in the period from the 1950s through the 1970s. As discussed in the introduction, there has been a recent resurgence in interest among art historians in these topics and the era of their emergence, several of whom have noted that systems thinking suffuses the art world today.[3] It is beyond the scope of the present discussion to describe the many

4. Walter De Maria, *The Lightning Field*, 1977, long-term installation, Quemado, New Mexico. ©The Estate of Walter De Maria. Courtesy Dia Art Foundation, New York. Photo: John Cliett.
An array of 400 stainless steel poles arranged in a one kilometer by one mile grid mark the vast landscape and act as lightning attractors for severe late summer storms that are endemic to this landscape. An early precedent for the use of technological features to mark environmental patterns, this sculpture was conceived at a time during which energy, systems, and energy-based approaches to ecology were becoming prominent themes in art practices.

interpretations of systems thinking by the artists of that era, or by contemporary artists and historians who have traced its continuing influence, but several points regarding the impact of systems thinking on art are relevant to our argument.[4] First, systems-based art is not medium-specific, although electronic media such as film, video, computers, and other digital devices often play a primary role in it. Second, whereas some artists and designers have experimented with the notion of autonomous systems, whereby an "authorless" art is produced without any apparent concern for a perceiving subject, many others challenge this notion by involving participants directly in the work in such ways that their participation changes the outcome or effect.[5] Lastly, because systems are understood as the "crossover rubric between natural and artificial worlds," systems thinking is fundamentally cross-disciplinary and can foster intersections among art, design, the life sciences, and engineering.[6] We will present some brief examples of mid-century art as essential background for our elucidation of how cybernetics and systems thinking remains present in contemporary work.

The Cybernetic Influence

Cybernetics is the study of control and communication in systems. Systems theory focuses on the elements and structure that define a system, and cybernetics focuses on how a system functions.[7] As noted in the introduction, cybernetics refers to self-regulating feedback loops, whereby an action or event triggers a change that is fed back into the system, thereby causing a change in the system, and so on in a recursive manner.

Throughout the 1960s, the Massachusetts Institute of Technology (MIT) was a significant locus for a group of scientists and artists invested in systems thinking. Cybernetics founder Norbert Wiener was a mathematics professor there

Dynamic Patterns: Visualizing Landscapes in a Digital Age

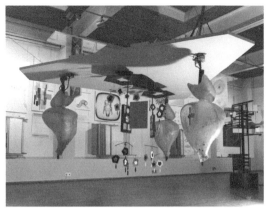

from 1919 to 1960;[8] artist György Kepes founded the Center for Advanced Visual Studies (CAVS), which would become a vehicle for collaboration among artists, architects, planners, scientists, and humanists, in 1967;[9] art critic Jack Burnham, who wrote the influential essay "Systems Esthetics" (1968), was a fellow at CAVS in 1969; and cyberneticist Gordon Pask was, in the 1970s, part of Nicholas Negroponte's Architecture Machine Group, which later became the MIT Media Lab. Two landmark exhibits introduced elsewhere around the close of the decade highlighted systems in art: *Cybernetic Serendipity: The Computer and the Arts* (London, 1968) and Burnham's *Software, Information Technology: Its New Meaning for Art* (New York, 1970), which was staged during the year after his fellowship at CAVS.[10] Rather than concentrating on individual objects *per se*, the works shown in these exhibits focused on feedback and communication among objects and their environments, often emphasizing the external conditions of a piece, such as people interfacing with it.[11]

To give one example, Pask's *Colloquy of Mobiles*, which was exhibited in *Cybernetic Serendipity*, consisted of five mobiles that interacted with each other through mirrors and flashlights. Light beams from "male" mobiles were aimed at rotating mirrors in "female" mobiles; when the light struck a mirror, it was reflected back to sensors near the male mobile, which briefly locked the mobiles together in equilibrium.[12] Exhibition visitors were given mirrors and lights to participate in this feedback loop, disrupt the "autonomy" of the mobiles, and thereby participate in a dance of humans and machines.[13]

Though the exhibition was largely lauded at the time of its opening, some warned of its acritical nature, noting that the curatorial position seemed to be concerned primarily with the celebration of technological developments that verged on entertainment and spectacle rather than considering the broader human potential or perils of such developments.[14] Irrespective of the inclusion of public participation in works of art, some historians have recently argued that the American art scene was characterized by an increasing positivism during the 1960s.[15] Even a project such as *Fun Palace*, conceived in

5. Gordon Pask, *Colloquy of Mobiles*, ICA London, 1968.

6. Philip Beesley, *Hylozoic Ground*, 2010. The Hylozoic series resemble life-like entities—an amalgam of creatures that seem both alien and familiar. Constructed using geotextiles embedded with microprocessors and sensors that activate chemical reactions in response to motion, the installations appear to breathe and their feather-like appendages stroke visitors and track their movements.

Behavioral Patterns

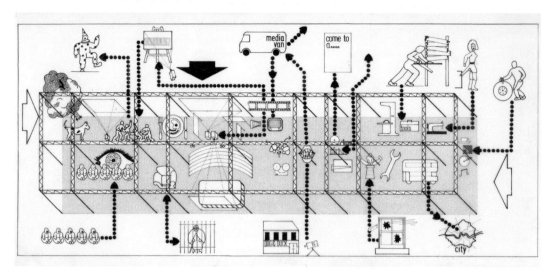

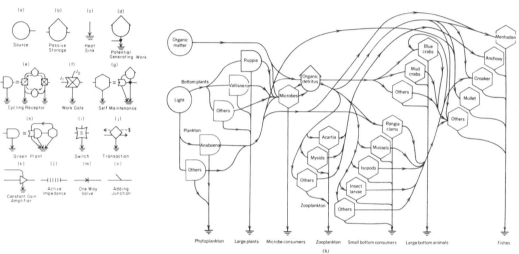

7. Cedric Price, *Inter-Action Centre*,
1977. Black ink, graphite and
adhesive screentone sheet on paper,
28.1cm x 60.1cm.
Similar to Fun Palace, this project
explored themes of indeterminacy,
flexibility, temporality, and the merging
of architecture and information
technologies.

8. Howard T. Odum, 1971.

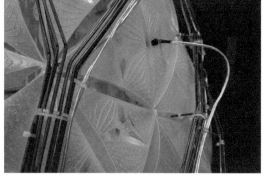

1961, could be seen in this light. For this work, Pask and his collaborators, architect Cedric Price and theater director Joan Littlefield, were interested in temporality, indeterminacy, and maximizing flexibility — ideas very pertinent to contemporary systems thinking. They believed that, because users could determine the building's configuration via movable walls, platforms, and escalators, the building would, in turn, "learn" users' patterns and continuously adapt to them. There was, however, a contradiction in this desire to anticipate behavior. As Pask's diagram of the project illustrates, "unmodified people" enter the building and "modified" people exit. The machine learned from their actions, so as to become increasingly efficient through cycles of prediction and evaluation. Though Price saw the project as a means to empower individuals to create their own environment, Pask's approach suggests a social-control machine that would evolve into a configuration to produce maximum happiness (i.e., modified people).[16] Furthermore, Burnham, who coined the phrase "systems aesthetics," came to question systems thinking and its emphasis on control. In 1974, he stated that "In terms of practical application, its utilitarianism and obsession with efficiency leave much about organic relationships misunderstood. Ultimately systems theory may be another attempt by science to resist the emotional pain and ambiguity that remain an unavoidable aspect of life."[17] The apprehension about whether systems thinking and information technologies represent increased mechanization and control of people and environments, or whether they facilitate individual agency that can challenge such control, remains with us today, as the answer depends on who has control and for what ends.

Notwithstanding this concern, Burnham's initial conception of systems aesthetics holds great potential for systems thinking beyond problem solving and control, and his early statements remain relevant today. In 1968, he declared that "The systems approach goes beyond a concern with staged environments and happenings; it deals in a revolutionary fashion with the larger problem of *boundary concepts*" (emphasis added).[18] Burnham later explained that he was interested

9. ecoLogicStudio, *METAfolly*, 2013. Rendering.
Constructed from waste material (recycled plastic panels, salvaged speakers from greeting card electronics, and LEDs), this folly uses information technology to remix virtual sounds with the real-time sounds and movements of people and animals interacting with the folly. This promiscuous interplay between real and virtual entities both fosters and disrupts communication between the technological and the living.

10. *METAfolly*. Detail.

Behavioral Patterns

11. Olafur Eliasson, *The Weather Project,* Tate Modern, London, 2003. Monofrequency lights, projection foil, haze machines, mirror foil, aluminum, scaffolding, 26.7m x 22.3m x 155.44m.

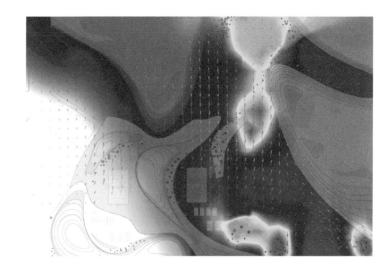

in work that "attempt[ed] to produce aesthetic sensations without the intervening 'object.'"[19] This conception of boundary without object is central to understanding behavioral patterns. In such patterns, boundaries are not stable lines of demarcation, but are spatially, temporally, materially, and conceptually malleable.

Boundary Concepts

One important reason for the recent resurgence of interest in systems thinking within art and design is the rapid expansion of digital technologies, including ever-increasing data collection capacity, the development of visualization software, and progressively greater computer power. These advances have paralleled major theoretical transformations in terms of how we understand ourselves in relation to our environment. Whereas early cybernetics relied on a machine model of nature, with humans looking in from outside, today we see a range of narratives and terminologies that run counter to this division. These narratives concern the flows and accumulations in which we are entangled but of which we are often unaware owing to the microscopic and macroscopic scales at which they take place and the temporal spans within which they occur. Descriptions of the relation between organism and environment have expanded beyond local or discrete entities. We have seen a shift away from characterizing humans as unique and individual organisms and toward understanding our confraternity with and dependence on other beings, including the trillions of organisms that live in and on our bodies. There is even an impetus to grant legal personhood to nonhuman primates. Visual and textual languages are emerging to describe these conditions, such as the now-prevalent term "Anthropocene," which was conceived to designate a new geological epoch in which human activities are the greatest force of environmental change.[20] Additionally, such concepts as "post-humanism,"

12. Sean Lally/Weathers, *Vatnsmýri Urban Planning*, Reykjavik, 2007. Drawing on the geothermal resources endemic to the region, this proposal uses heat as a design medium. By strategically funneling underground thermal energy to the surface, a series of connected microclimates could extend outdoor activity in colder months. The shifting patterns of activity are a register of the invisible heat field buried deep beneath the surface.

Behavioral Patterns

13. Diller, Scofidio + Renfro,
Blur Building, Yverdon-les-Bains,
Switzerland, 2002.
Built for the Swiss Expo, the building's
"façade" is a continually shifting cloud
that is responsive to its environment.
Mist envelops the scaffold as water is
drawn from the lake through pressurized
nozzles that are regulated in response to
temperature, humidity, and wind speed.
The designers intended for visitors to
wear "braincoats" that would match
visitor information so that a colored
blush would appear on the coat as
visitors with similar interests came
near each other. Cary Wolfe describes
this project as a brilliant example of
a system-environment reformulation
owing to its "unstable form" and refusal
to produce a fixed image. Similarly,
the designers hoped to challenge the
expectation that technological displays,
which are endemic to Expos, be used
in the name of efficiency and use them
instead for indeterminate effects.

"species thinking," "agents," "assemblages," and "hyperobjects" have been coined or used to describe these conditions and environments.[21]

These concepts address relationships and behaviors among multiple entities, particularly those having to do with human–nonhuman relations and nature–culture definitions. Bruno Latour, for example, asks why we tend to speak of "cultures" in the plural but "nature" in the singular and calls for art practices to help us conceive of hybrid natures–cultures that can define ecological thinking for today.[22] Philosopher Timothy Morton argues that the nature–culture dialectic is based on reconciliation with a nature that does not, and perhaps never did, exist; he suggests that it would be better to imagine "ecology without a *concept* of the natural."[23] Philosopher Cary Wolfe reinforces these critiques, stating that "the environment is not simply 'given' (that would land us back into a thinly disguised concept of nature in the traditional sense) but is in a crucial sense *produced*."[24] To understand behavioral patterns through a system–environment framework, we must not define the concept of environment generally or singularly, despite the importance of pleas to "save *the* environment"; rather, we must recognize the presence of many environments, each described through a particular frame of reference, which means that each is demarcated by a different set of boundary conditions.

Such conditions can be made evident through particular modes of representation, including language. As media theorist Marshall McLuhan argued, new media *are* new environments, and the artist's role includes using such media to create what he termed "anti-environments."[25] He reasoned that we

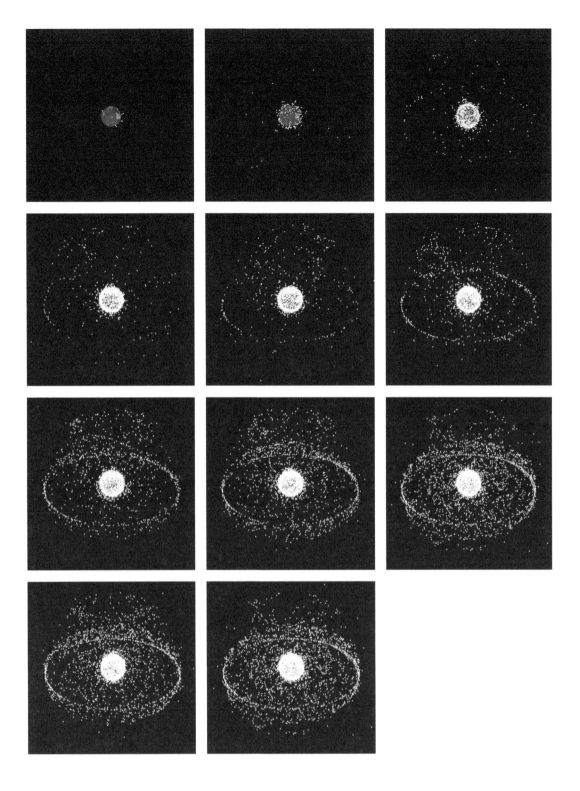

14. NASA orbital debris simulations, 1960–2010, demonstrate the tremendous increase in the amount of orbital debris. Ninety-five percent of objects circling the Earth are non-functional satellites.

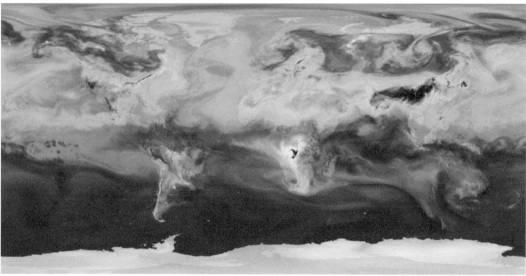

15. Stills taken from NASA's GEOS-5
"Nature Run" computer model,
which captures how carbon dioxide
circulates around the globe over one
year. The simulation illustrates both
the dispersion of greenhouse gases
from their source and the dramatic
shift in carbon dioxide levels caused by
seasonal vegetation change.

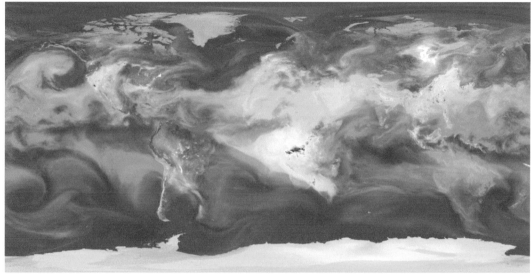

cannot perceive an environment until we create another one with which to conscribe it. In a prescient 1967 statement, McLuhan theorized that artists would create anti-environments on a planetary scale:

> If the planet itself has thus become the content of a new space created by its satellites, and its electronic extensions, if the planet has become the content and not the environment, then we can confidently expect to see the next few decades devoted to turning the planet into an art form. We will caress and shape and pattern every facet, every contour of this planet as if it were a work of art, just as surely as we have put a new environment around it. I think the computer is admirably suited to the artistic programming of such an environment.[26]

The realization of this statement is evident in the various mappings of global phenomena that we see today—tracking the flow of goods, carbon dioxide concentration, weather, or air traffic—many of which are drawn to show temporal changes and patterns that are not otherwise visible. Thus, a key aspect of these types of patterns is that they cannot be seen by the human eye but only through a technological medium, specifically information technologies that use such devices as motion and heat sensors and satellites to capture data that are then translated into legible patterns.

The extent to which sensing and digital devices have permeated our world may have been underestimated by even the most ardent supporters of early computer technology, though systems art was never limited to any particular technology; its focus was instead on using various apparatuses to discover new patterns. Kepes was the most ardent champion of the potential of optical and data technologies to create a new visual language that could bring together art and science. He believed that instruments such as remote sensors and data monitors could be used to convey knowledge about pollution and other environmental conditions to the urban populace, thereby revealing aspects of the environment that would otherwise remain hidden. He argued that data from multiple sources could be combined to make visible "the changing characteristics of the environmental 'common'" and that such a display "could be instrumental in developing a civic consciousness of problems that concern everyone."[27] Kepes hoped that new technologies would be used imaginatively to develop an "ecological consciousness," in part through an artistic exploration of patterns and processes.[28] The main thrust of Kepes's argument in *The New Landscape* (1956) as well as his introduction to *Arts of the Environment*, "Art and Ecological Consciousness" (1972), was to exploit technologies for their ability to reveal patterns across scales. In the earlier book, Kepes stated, "In a sequence from the very large to the very small, a world of sense patterns, is projected which contains spatial and temporal structures different from anything to which men are accustomed."[29]

Cutting-edge technologies that were unavailable to Kepes sixty years ago have made this world of sense patterns even more accessible and have given rise to new forms of ecological consciousness in light of our current environmental preoccupations, such as global warming, ozone depletion, and toxins, the long term trends of which are imperceptible except through the data reported by our observational instruments. Such tools alter the domain of what we know and, therefore, how and where we might intervene.[30] Kepes believed that a visual language of patterns could bridge science and art, just as McLuhan believed in the importance of pattern recognition as a means to achieve environmental awareness; for both, new tools of observation were essential for bringing forth these invisible environments.[31] This expansion of knowledge creation, however, does not call for unbridled optimism. The unease over the quantification, optimization, and control that characterized early systems thinking has been exacerbated by the proliferation of tracking and surveillance technologies infiltrating our lives, often with little democratic oversight. "Big data," "smart cities," and the "internet of things" can be used to produce more efficient systems, such as reducing

16. **PEG office of landscape +
architecture,** *Smog Urchin,* Taichung
Gateway Park, 2011.
The urchin is indexical in two ways:
first, its position traces the path of the
runway of this former airport; second,
its material is a filament that neutralizes
pollutants and changes color depending
on air quality.

carbon emissions or optimizing traffic flow; however, critics
note that these developments, which are being stimulated by
corporations like IBM and Samsung, risk reducing reality to
a single, technological narrative that homogenizes the differences of how such technologies are employed in various
applications and in different parts of the world.[32] Addressing
the question of who has access to and control of this information is more vital than ever.[33]

  Despite these significant challenges, there remains
the potential to engage systems thinking in ways that neither
blindly celebrate information technologies nor claim to solve
the problems that these technologies can ably represent.
Rather, such tools offer ways to create aesthetic sensibilities
that tap into our broader recognition of the embeddedness
of humans within the many natures that characterize our environments, near and far. This observation is consistent with
McLuhan's argument that we cannot see an environment until
a new one encircles it—a condition that is enabled when
new media arise. These considerations raise such questions as
how these media might be used to imagine new "boundary
concepts" with respect to nature–culture, body–environment,
or human–nonhuman entities, how sensor and tracking technologies can be utilized to create an awareness of the patterns
that pervade our world, and whether this awareness might shed
light on environmental matters of concern.[34]

Agents, Interactions, and Feedback

In our introduction to this book, we described the influence
of systems thinking on contemporary landscape architecture in
terms of how emergence has been interpreted through the
lens of ecological concepts. Though this notion of emergence
assumes feedback processes within an ecosystem (i.e., how it
evolves or persists), the design work inspired by this idea is
often interpreted in such a way as to presume a linear progres-
sion of natural systems toward states of greater complexity.
Rarely do the projects focus on feedback *per se*; instead, they
presume a minimal or noninterventionist approach once natural

processes are set in motion. The projects in this chapter, by contrast, are concerned with the feedback part of the process. This latter approach is more reminiscent of landscape architect Lawrence Halprin's use of cybernetic ideas in the development of his notational system of "scores" in the 1960s, as discussed in the previous chapter, in which performance focused on human interaction and involvement.

Michael Ezban's *Saturation Scenarios* (2015) is an agent-based model that simulates the effects of fluctuating water levels at Owens Lake in southeastern California, a desiccated lakebed that was created when the lake's waters were diverted to Los Angeles. Owens Lake is considered the largest source of dust pollution in the United States, and is responsible for lung disease and increased cancer rates among local residents. To minimize hazards from wind-borne carcinogenic particulates, various dust control measures have been instituted, including the use of bubblers to saturate more than 35 square miles of the flat, salt-crusted lakebed with shallow ponds and sheets of water.[35] Algae growth in these brackish saturation zones feeds large volumes of brine flies and brine shrimp, which in turn provide a rich food source for over one hundred different species of migratory shorebirds and waterfowl. Inadvertently, this remediation strategy has created a significant bird habitat that now offers a flourishing resource for bird watchers and photographers.[36]

Ezban's drawings, which consist of the output from a model that he encoded, index the entanglements among these various agents. Though not structured as a true time-scale simulation, the model approximates the range of saturation scenarios that occur over a typical nine-month wetting season. Eight points (blue crosses) represent the array of bubbler zones distributed throughout the lake. At each point, interpolated flow rate and duration data from the Los Angeles Power and Water Department were used to produce radii of varied size and duration (orange circles). The dynamic mosaic derived from these overlapping saturation zones was of particular importance given the likelihood that areas in these zones would have the greatest potential for increased wetland plant and waterfowl

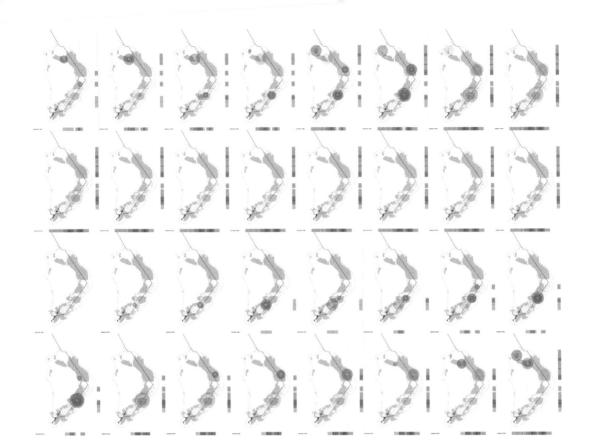

17. Michael Ezban, *Saturation Scenarios*,
Owens Lake, CA, 2015.
Drawing output from an agent-based
simulation.

18. *Saturation Scenarios.* Drawing
enlargement.

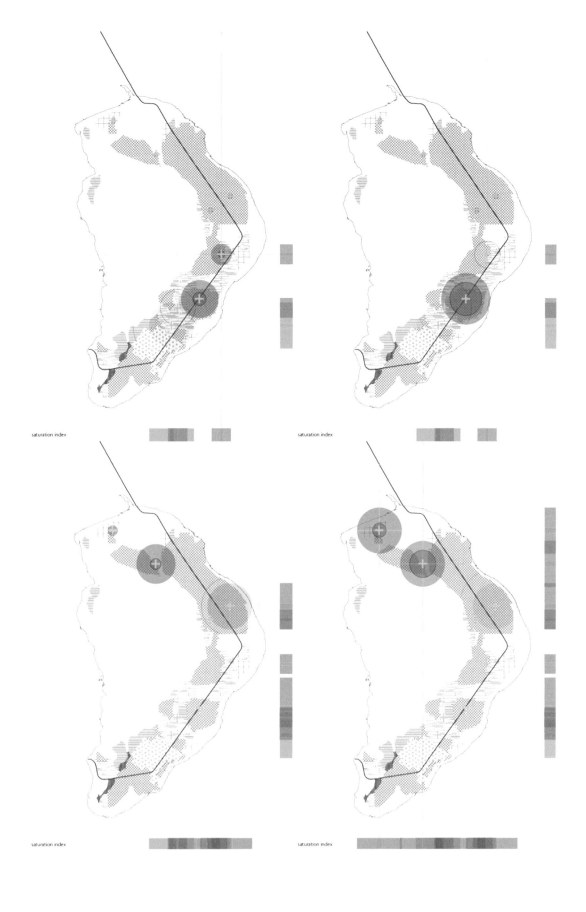

saturation index

saturation index

saturation index

saturation index

19. Natalie Jeremijenko (The
Environmental Health Clinic) and David
Benjamin (The Living), *Amphibious
Architecture*, installation in East and
Bronx Rivers, NY, 2009.

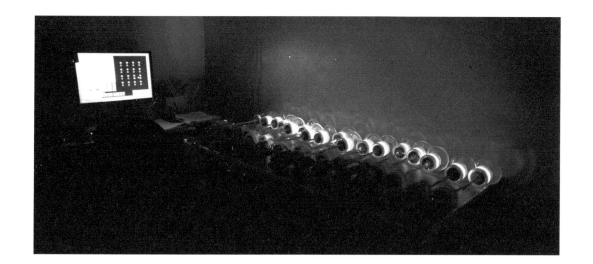

population growth. Adjustments to the model's flow rate and duration resulted in simulations that illustrated the shifting spatial and material conditions that have occurred and, importantly, signaled new locations for future remediation and recreation zones that can be used to inform the management of ecotourism sites.[37]

This method, which models actions among a number of interrelated entities, could be developed as an interface that displays the relationships among the many factors constituting the ever-changing environment around the lake. As climate change renders water supplies increasingly variable, the shifting boundaries and loci of agent–environment relations in the simulations highlight the need to grapple with the complexities of our greatly altered water systems, the effects of which are both highly local and broadly diffuse. Additionally, the project provides an important conceptual framework for interpreting how we might understand habitat restoration. Here, it is not a recovery of what the draining of Owens Lake destroyed, but a new discovery and valuing of the natures that have taken its place—that is, of plants and animals now thriving in this place that has been greatly altered by humans.

In a similar manner, much of Natalie Jeremijenko's work, which she describes as organism-centric design, engages directly with nonhuman agents to create feedback among humans, animals, and environments. For example, *Amphibious Architecture* (2009), in collaboration with the design firm The Living, uses mobile media, sensors, and floating tubes (buoys) to which LED lights have been affixed. Installed in New York City's East and Bronx Rivers, the work features shifting colors and intensities of light that indicate changing water quality and the presence of fish. A text messaging interface enables people to receive water quality information from the buoys, and the lights indicate when fish are present so that people can feed them with a food that absorbs toxins. The "machinic" feature of this assemblage, wherein the parts have no inherent physical

20. *Amphibious Architecture.* Testing and development of the buoys.

Behavioral Patterns

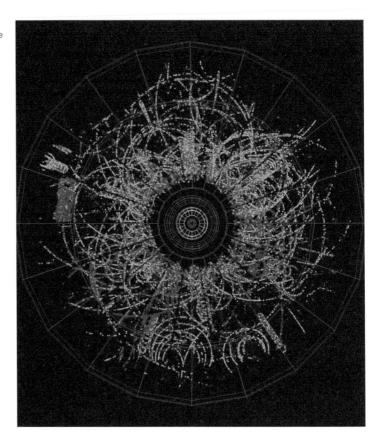

unity but still function together, renders visible the interdependence of humans and fish and their shared aquatic ecosystem and also engages individuals as agents of transformation. The feedback among sensor, signal, text, and food fashions a form of mutualism across species boundaries. Organisms, both humans and fish, recognize and respond to patterns, which can condition their actions when they are rewarded or otherwise reinforced.

Both *Saturation Scenarios* and *Amphibious Architecture* use multiple technologies, such as sequenced bubblers, simulation models, sensors, and SMS feeds, to relate the behavioral patterns of people and fluctuating environmental and animal patterns, using signals and feedback to mediate between them. In the latter project in particular, these tools enable a direct dialogue, which shifts a person's experience from reflection to active engagement.[38] Both projects offer compelling examples that recall Burnham's notion of producing sensations without intervening objects. Though these projects do contain many objects, including not only the aforementioned technologies but also animals, animal feed, water, and so on, the work does not exist in any of these objects themselves but in the changing behaviors and shifting boundaries that become manifest through the objects' relations with each other over time. The recursive nature of the media employed—sensing, processing, and acting—offers an expanded approach to engaging

processes in landscapes, particularly when such processes occur on temporal and spatial scales that are not directly perceptible to the naked eye, making it difficult for people to understand the changes taking place over time.

Dispersed Objects

> Direct perception of transformation evades us....
> We lack a visual vocabulary of change.[39]
> —György Kepes

> The pattern recognition that is quite impossible during processes of slow change, becomes quite easy when the same changes are speeded up even to movie or cinematic levels.[40]
> —Marshall McLuhan

22. Future Cities Lab, *Aurora Model*, New York, 2009.
The Aurora model is one piece of a three-part installation that highlights the interconnection between the remote and ephemeral dimensions of the Arctic Circle and the local, experiential space of the gallery. The model, embedded with sensors and LEDs, produces a fluctuating glow that is an index of both visitors' movements and real-time data of the Arctic ice field, linking the behavioral patterns of human bodies to the remote Arctic body of melting ice.

To understand change, we need indicators that register change and signs that we can interpret. Timothy Morton's notion of "hyperobjects," which is especially relevant to the problem of the imperceptibility of such change, was presaged by McLuhan's expectation that new environments would be conceptualized at the planetary scale as a means of giving legibility to environments as content rather than as background. Morton cites global warming and radioactive waste as quintessential

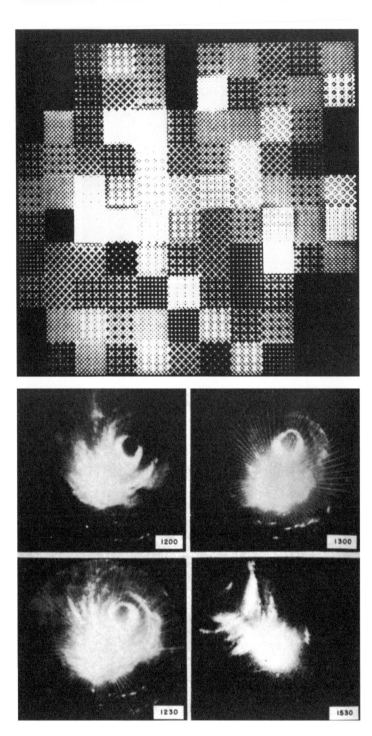

examples of hyperobjects because they are "massively distributed in time and space relative to humans" and "involve profoundly different temporalities than the human-scale ones we are used to."[41] Morton maintains that "climate change represents the possibility that the cycles and repetitions [patterns] we come to depend on for our sense of stability and place in the world may be the harbingers of cataclysmic change."[42] Advanced imaging tools may be the only way to access hyperobjects, and even then only partially, but they are largely responsible for the increased attention now being paid to macro-scale patterns and processes.[43] Designers are engaging hyperobjects precisely to bring them into view at a human scale and provide alternatives to the back-to-nature version of environmentalism that Morton denounces. The prominence of atmosphere and energy projects is noteworthy in this regard. Such projects attempt to link large-scale patterns, such as atmospheric changes or fluctuating energy use, to people's interactions with these systems at local and experiential levels.

A compelling example of a work that engages systems in multiple ways is Yusuke Obuchi's *Wave Garden* (2002), which was created as his architectural thesis at Princeton University. *Wave Garden* functions as both public space and power plant. The project exemplifies a current design interest in fusing energy infrastructure and public space while making their relationship mutually dependent in ways that go beyond simply conjoining environmental and recreational programs. It is conceived as a functioning power plant and simultaneously as a register of energy use, providing visual feedback about energy consumption via a flexible, floating membrane.

This 480-acre membrane, which Obuchi proposed locating in the ocean off the coast of southern California, contains 1800 individual modules that are connected but can move somewhat independently in response to wave action. The modules are made with a flexible material that produces energy by transforming the wave oscillation by means of piezoelectricity.[44] On weekdays, when the plant is in full production, the electricity generated by the membrane feeds the state's power grid. On the weekend, electric current is fed back to the

23. BELL Laboratories, 1966.
An early attempt to simulate the intensity and movement of a rain storm in Holmdel, NJ. Ninety-six gauges spread across fifty square miles recorded the rainfall in ten-second intervals. Each patch represents the rainfall volume through an increasing gradient of black (no rain) to white (heavy rain).

24. Time series of a typhoon captured by a US Navy ship's radar, 1944. This storm was the first tropical storm to be observed on radar.

25. Yusuke Obuchi, *Wave Garden*, Pacific
Ocean, CA, 2002. Location map and plan.

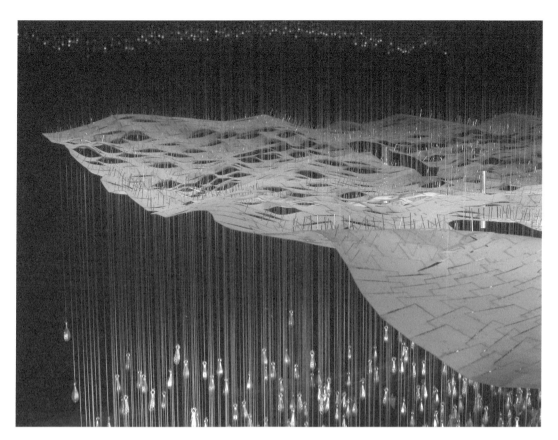

26. *Wave Garden*. Model detail.

membrane, causing it to deform into an inhabitable island. Modules are selectively elevated above the surface of the water, providing a canopy under which watercraft can gain access and through which visitors can move vertically to enter its upper surface. The amount of recreational space provided on the weekend is inversely proportional to the amount of energy consumed during the week; the less energy used during the week, the more canopy and accessible surface are available for recreation on weekends.[45] One could criticize this effect as unjustly punitive, since there is likely no correlation between the largest consumers of energy and the people seeking to access the membrane for recreation.

Despite this substantial concern, Obuchi's thesis on systems and cybernetics is thought-provoking. As a closed system, it is an energy circuit; as an open system, its configuration depends on the effect of people on the closed system by means of their weekly energy use. It is possible to imagine how the project might create constituencies advocating for energy conservation in order to maximize access to weekend recreation.

This project meets the criteria of a hyperobject distributed in time and space. It is imperceptible in its entirety, but its effects can be perceived.[46] Furthermore, *Wave Garden* achieves its effects by employing two kinds of pattern, one physical and one behavioral. As a physical form, the pattern (comprised of gridded modules) is unstable and shifting; as

27. Long exposure photograph of birds flocking.

a behavior, the pattern is neither stable nor unstable, neither physical nor locatable. Instead, the pattern is simply the *recognition* of the correlation between the two systems of energy and people, interacting over time.[47]

Saturation Scenarios, Amphibious Architecture, and *Wave Garden* all exemplify Gregory Bateson's conception of an art object that is itself patterned and also part of a larger patterned universe. Bateson's pronouncement, like McLuhan's notion of anti-environments, refers to a constellation of entities held together across time and space. Although these projects refer to particular locations, whether Owens Lake, the East and Bronx Rivers, or the Pacific Ocean, they are less focused on the site as a singular idea or location and more concerned with the exchanges occurring among multiple constituents.[48] In other words, these projects are ecological in the sense that Bateson meant when he stated that thinking ecologically means recognizing ourselves as part of the systems with which we interact.[49] As early as 1949, Bateson stated, "The scientist is not outside.... The scientist is part of the thing which he studies, as much as the artist. And it is that move—the discovery that the observer is a significant part of the thing observed—that marks the change of an epoch."[50] This premise has long been accepted in many fields, including landscape architecture; the projects described here, however, make the "observer" an active participant in shaping the work in ways that are distinct from how we typically understand the engagement of people with processes in the landscape. *Saturation Scenarios* and *Amphibious Architecture*, in particular, communicate about and with nature(s) in an ongoing exchange among humans, wildlife, and our shared environment.

Conclusion: Revealing the Invisibles

> Clearly, the artist's sensibility has entered a new
> phase of orientation in which its prime goal is
> to provide a format for the emerging ecological
> consciousness.[51]
> —György Kepes

The behavioral patterns described above are the progeny of
mid-century systems-based art in that they are multimedia,
engage participation in ways that change the outcome or form
of the work itself, and are crossovers between "natural" and
"artificial" worlds. These are promising directions for thinking
about feedback and its relationship to behavior in less auto-
cratic ways than some of the early proponents of cybernetics,
who posited parallels between mind and machine. Such a view
was initially presumed to be free of ideology; the organizational
equivalence observed among the networks that characterize
human brains, cities, and societies was simply seen as a scientific (i.e., "objective") idea that could be used to understand
the organization of both social and natural systems.[52] Some
mid-century artists, however, followed a more open interpretation of systems theory; like Bateson, they were critical of an
approach that viewed nature and people as closed and autonomous cybernetic machines.[53] The ongoing relevance of systems
thinking in contemporary art and design, indicated by exhibitions, symposia, and numerous publications, tends to follow this
latter thread.[54]

   It nevertheless remains critical to ask whether the
emphasis on behavioral patterns risks expanding technocratic
control, as has been recently argued regarding Kepes's work,
or if pattern-seeing offers a framework for understanding relationships without assuming an authoritative hand.[55] It is impossible to answer this question in general terms. Even works
authored by the same group of individuals can be seen as contradictory in their ambitions. Some projects appear to empower
people with knowledge and the ability to affect the systems

28. Chris Jordan, *Midway: Message from the Gyre*, 2009–current.
A photograph of one of many dead juvenile albatrosses found in the Midway Atoll, a cluster of islands over 2000 miles from the nearest continent. The young birds are fed plastic foraged by their parents from the vast amounts of debris in the Pacific Ocean. The artist states that "the mythical albatross calls upon us to recognize that our greatest challenge lies not out there, but in here."

29. Debris in Kanapou Bay, Hawaii.

with which they are engaging, whereas other projects gather information in ways that have the obvious potential for misuse or that contribute to the belief that more data simply equals more knowledge or answers. Designers can play an important role by deriving alternative representations that are not based on optimizing single criteria; rather, representations can be made by using the same tools and techniques, but to different ends.[56] Thus it remains important to continually ask for whom these patterns of information are organized.

There is room for much more exploration in this realm. In the best cases, attention to behavioral patterns is not directed toward maximizing efficiency or valorizing data visualization; rather, this approach concentrates on revealing processes and events that occur at scales beyond our immediate perception, thereby bringing them into focus.[57] As seen through McLuhan's media ecology, our collective engagement with our environments is shaped by and through new informational media.[58] Our understanding is therefore dependent upon the constitution of the semiotic systems employed in the transfer of information among these media; such systems enable us to tap into otherwise invisible relationships in order to increase our perception of the patterns that connect.

Ornamental Patterns

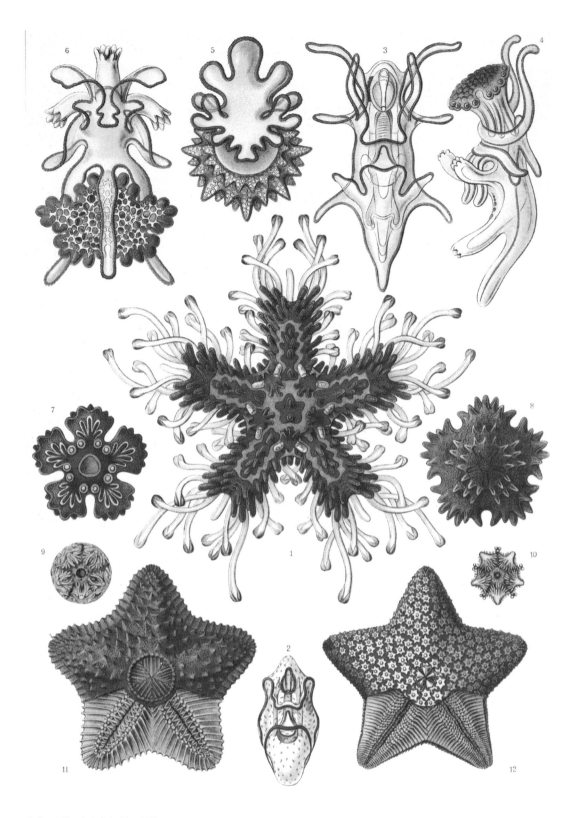

1. Ernst Haeckel, *Asteridea*, 1899.
Plate of Asteridea (starfish) arranged in
symmetrical composition.

In the past two decades, there has been a proliferation of patterned surfaces. Numerous publications in the field of architecture have theorized about the reasons behind this surge, and there is disagreement as to whether these patterned surfaces constitute ornament as it has been historically understood, particularly in terms of its relationship to utility. There is also disagreement about how ornament differs from pattern, or whether ornament is simply a subset of pattern. To us, it is clear that not all ornaments involve pattern (consider statuaries, for example), nor are all surface patterns ornamental (a grid, for example). However, a type of ornament can be generated through pattern-making whereby surfaces are structured using repetitive geometries that undergo a visible transformation, such as rotation or reflection, or apply recognizable motifs in a recurring fashion. The repetition afforded by parametric software and CNC machines has facilitated this rapid rise in pattern-making. Though technology alone does not create design innovation, new tools facilitate new techniques that open up design exploration and imagination.

Regardless of what is considered ornament, some commentators suggest that the abundance of patterned surfaces is rooted in the quest for "legibility."[1] We have sought, in this book, to describe that pursuit by foregrounding pattern as the connection between natural processes and human perception of those processes. As we have argued throughout, sensory and aesthetic functions, by way of pattern-finding and pattern-forming, should play a much larger role in defining an ecological ethos for landscape design. This chapter examines how ornamental patterns participate in the expression of that ethos and explains how these expressions differ from the patterns previously described. Since the geometrical transformations and icons characteristic of ornamental patterns are meant to be legible *on the surface* of a building or landscape, some might consider them the most "superficial" type of pattern; however, ornament — through the process of pattern-making — is not separate from organization but is what gives rise to it.

Ornamental patterns have appeared in gardens throughout history. A quintessential example is the

2. The Privy Garden at Hampton Court Palace c. 1702.
Throughout time and cultures geometric patterns have held symbolic significance representing human's terrestrial relationship to a greater natural and divine order.

3. Matthew Ritchie and Aranda\Lasch, *The Evening Line,* aluminum, epoxy, vinyl, video, 2008.
The structure, based on a scalable, fractal geometry, transitions between two and three dimensions.

4. Martha Schwartz, *Garden Ornaments*, Dörentrup, Germany, 2001.
A temporary installation of fifty-one popular garden ornaments, each sitting on a white box. The boxes were arranged in a grid so as to impose a pattern on the landscape. Like minimalism and pop art, influences that Schwartz has acknowledged, the technique of repetition is a framing function that enables us to see these objects in a different way.

parterre—geometrically intricate, symmetrical figures created with low hedges or groundcover—that peaked in the seventeenth-century French baroque garden. Ornamental patterns are also present in eighteenth- and nineteenth-century pattern books, the mid-twentieth-century work of Roberto Burle Marx, the work of Martha Schwartz in the 1980s and 1990s, and in many practices today, including Workshop: Ken Smith Landscape Architect, West 8, and Gross Max. Even so, none of these recent practices has positioned its work under the rubric of ornament *per se*, nor have others attempted to do so. In fact, the subject of ornament has not been addressed theoretically in contemporary landscape design, and, on those occasions when it is acknowledged, the references are often disparaging. There is considerable skepticism about surface, as evidenced by the amount of attention paid to a landscape's practical and measurable functions, often while overlooking its formal attributes. This chapter, by contrast, considers how ornamental patterns can serve as a vehicle through which to "communicate" landscape functions. The use of ornamental patterns to achieve a melding of utility and sign may invite criticism because, by many definitions, ornament is explicitly intended to function in ways that are purely symbolic rather than useful or measurable. This dualism is characteristic of the binary thinking that often shapes discussions about ornament.[2] However, a slightly longer view of the history of ornament shows that its relation to utility has frequently been one of association rather than opposition.

Ornament and Utility

The differences of opinion regarding ornament's relationship to utility are epitomized in a 2008 article by architecture critic Robert Levit, who maintains that contemporary ornament has resurfaced within architectural discourse "by putting behind

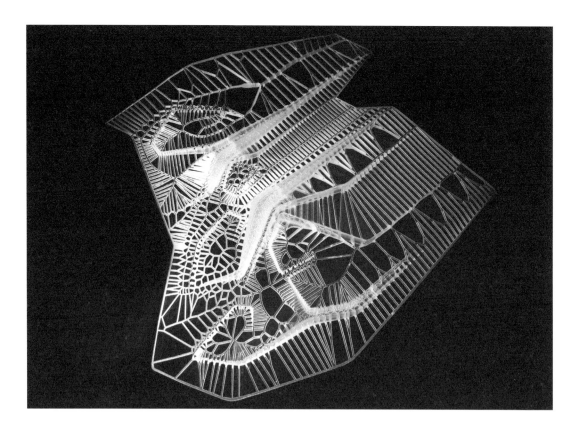

5. Tom Wiscombe, *Garak Market*, Seoul, 2009. Digital model of roof structure/garden.
The roof structure was derived using principles inspired by an earlier study of the morphology of dragonfly wings, which exhibit structural properties of rigidity (ladder-like patterns) and flexibility (honeycomb patterns). The resulting hybrid is that of a beam-membrane amalgamation.

what gave it its past notoriety: its position outside of instrumental need, which is to say, its openly symbolic nature."[3] Levit strongly disagrees with this position. His article is a critique of Farshid Moussavi and Michael Kubo's *Function of Ornament*, a book that aims primarily to liberate ornament from its association with either symbolic form or surface decoration.[4] According to Moussavi and Kubo, if ornament is to be relevant today, it must be based on patterns that participate in functions, such as lighting control and structure. They argue that buildings cannot communicate through traditional representational means, through which architects try to *produce* signification, but only through experience and sensation, which circumvent the need for a codified language.[5] Levit, by contrast, contends that ornament "can never be reduced to a question of function and is incompatible as a category with that which simply functions or is the product of the technical logic of construction or craftsmanship."[6] He holds that the category of ornament has emerged historically only owing to the recognition of form as symbolic.[7]

Levit outlines the myriad misgivings expressed by architects regarding symbolic practices. These concerns range from criticisms that understanding symbols requires a high degree of familiarity with their origins and that, therefore, they are not discernible to the broader public, to the objection that the use of symbols risks being replicated as superficial add-ons, stylistic imitation, and kitsch, attributes for which some

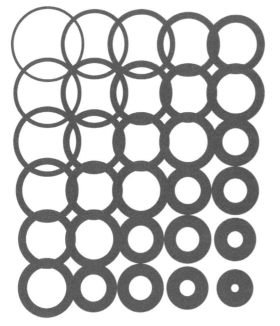
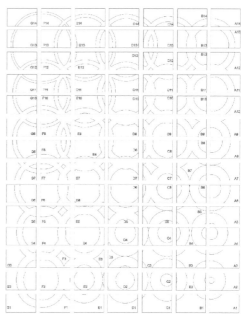

6. PEG office of landscape + architecture, *Not Garden*, 2009, Philadelphia. An experimental landscape maintenance strategy using geotextile to grow patterns on vacant lots. Initial installation (left) and growth after one year.

7. *Not Garden*. Drawing showing the templates used for cutting the geotextile.

postmodernist work has been criticized. This latter concern is the primary reason that Moussavi and others have reframed ornament in terms of sensation and "affect," albeit produced through functional criteria, and distanced it from its role in representation and signification.[8] In any case, Levit notes that a redefinition of ornament under a functional rubric simply "participates in a long Modernist tradition that would like to uncouple building from symbolic practices—to make buildings simply real."[9] We strongly agree with his assessment that ornament—or any form for that matter—cannot be reduced to a question of utilitarian function. We do, however, agree with Moussavi that ornament can be used in conjunction with utility, as has often occurred in the past.

Historically, beauty and ornamentation were inseparable, as were utility and ornamentation. Ornament was the means to tie together surface and structure, style and function, or the universal (recognizable symbols, cosmos, nature) and the particular (the manifestation of the universal in specific forms and materials and in specific locales or cultures). Current dictionaries describe ornament as "a way to make something look more attractive and less plain," "a mere outward display," and define it as synonymous with "embellish," which is "to enhance the appearance of something by adding something unessential." These common definitions all point to ornament as a decorative add-on. According to other definitions, however, ornament is "an accessory, article, or detail used to beautify the appearance of something to which it is added or *of which it is a part* (emphasis added)," and some historical definitions describe ornament as that which occurs between something that is necessary, such as a structural support, and that which has no utility.[10] During the Roman Imperial era, ornament was legally defined as an element that was affixed to a structure but could be detached from it, making it neither as immovable as the structure itself nor as portable as furniture.[11] It was later defined as something "superadded to utility."[12] The question of whether ornament is supplementary thus lies at the root of its definition, a duality that is embedded in the word itself. Its etymology is from the Latin *ornamentum*, which means "apparatus, equipment, trappings; embellishment, decoration, trinket"; however, it also shares its root with the verb *ordo*, "to order." Architectural historian Antoine Picon notes that the kinship between ornament and order is similar to that shared by the words *cosmos* and *cosmetic*, derived from the Greek word *kosmein*, "to adorn"; both pairs of terms denote an all-encompassing order as well as its embellishment.[13]

In landscape architecture today, ornament is widely perceived as something unessential that wrongly privileges vision over multi-sensory immersion. Elizabeth K. Meyer, for example, defines beauty (which she values) in opposition to ornamentation or to visual and formal effects. She argues compellingly that beauty and aesthetics must be incorporated into sustainability agendas and criticizes those who dismiss beauty as a superficial concern.[14] She goes on to say that many landscape architects equate "beauty and aesthetics with the visual and the formal, and in doing so render them inconsequential … [and blind] to the distinctions between beauty and

> 8. Loktak Lake in northeast India. Phumdis are naturally occurring mats of organic matter. The circular shapes in this image have been artificially created with phumdis for use in fish farming.

beautification or ornamentation."[15] Others have argued that landscape architecture should be renamed "landscape science" in a bid to leave behind architectural concerns, defined as surface and program, for the "deeper" work based on knowledge of soils and geology, among other skills. Such a repositioning, it is argued, would enable designers of landscapes to be systematic in their work and to distinguish between "surface and substance, appearance and essence."[16] We do not disagree with the importance of material or scientific knowledge but, again, believe that surface is here unnecessarily positioned in opposition to the materiality and functionality of landscapes.[17] As we noted in the introduction, both Gregory Bateson and György Kepes warned against such dichotomous thinking, which favors quantitative knowledge because it is considered "real" while devaluing qualitative concerns. This thinking is rooted in a modernist view that sees ornament as a superfluous imposition on the landscape, unresponsive to the specifics of a site and its program.

Ornament and Style

By style people meant ornamentation.[18]
—Adolf Loos (1910)

The "styles" are a lie.[19]
—Le Corbusier (1923)

In Western cultures, ornament was banished for a significant part of the twentieth century. It was considered an outdated form of expression, irrelevant in light of emerging technologies of mass production, and excessive in view of the social needs of the majority. Once affiliated with imperialism, religion, and colonialism, ornament came to be seen as a representation of individual class and wealth. As it became associated with taste and social "correctness" (décor, decorum, decoration), ornament lost its agency.[20] Some critics of ornament believed that the modern lack of decoration was a "middle-class trait to be celebrated for its rejection of aristocratic pomp and representation of status."[21]

Architect Adolf Loos is best known for his fervent dismissal of ornament in his 1908 lecture "Ornament and Crime." Several decades later, Christopher Tunnard, in his influential *Gardens in the Modern Landscape* (1938), cited Loos's famous quote: "Progress in taste goes hand in hand with the elimination of ornament in everyday things."[22] Rejecting ornament as irrelevant and wasteful, Tunnard, along with American mid-twentieth-century landscape architects Garrett Eckbo, Dan Kiley, and James Rose, adapted functionalist arguments from architecture to modern landscape design. Tunnard went so far as to call ornament deceitful: "Ornamentation has in itself a suggestion of disguise, of what is, in fact, a tangible form of lying and … the decoration of useful objects is a confession of failure in [the] original design."[23] He argued that the use of ornament would naturally wane with a proper emphasis on efficiency and that functional planning "automatically becomes that which is good and the need for space filling or accentuating decoration disappears."[24] In this view, ornament is seen as something *applied to* the site rather than *derived from* it. Along the same lines, James Rose endorsed a more efficient use of plant material by maintaining that massing plants together to define space was "unscientific." He argued that the use of individual specimens was more resourceful because all sides of a plant are used, resulting in the need for fewer plants.[25] Calling for a minimalist aesthetic, Rose claimed, "Ornamentation with plants in landscape design to create 'pictures' or picturesque effect means what ornamentation has always meant: the fate call of an outworn system of aesthetics."[26]

Despite the harsh rhetoric, however, ornament did not disappear altogether from modernism. Rather than being expressed via historical styles, ornament was articulated through the careful use of materials with inherent patterns, or as an outward expression of underlying structure.[27] Thus, for example, Thomas Beeby suggested in 1977 that ornament had

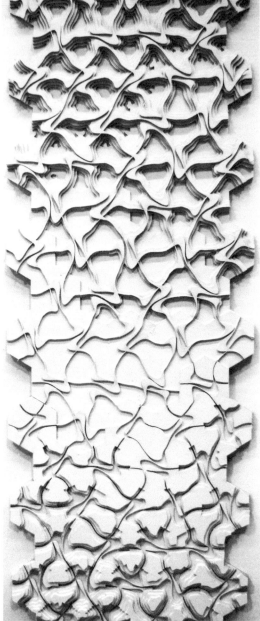

9. Joshua Freese, 2016.
Computer-generated surface
transformation based on hexagonal
geometry.

10. Francisco Allard, 2009, laser cut
model. The underlying organization is
a drawing of uniform hexagons with
interior shapes. The topographic surface
of the model is created by altering the
elevation of the hexagons in a non-
uniform manner.

found its way into the organization of urban form and buildings, in that a basic grid or proportioning system was
set in place to control the manipulation of elements for ornamental purposes.[28] According to Beeby, the only types of
ornament rejected by Loos and others were those that were
historically derived and applied independent of structure or
composition. In other words, even though ornament cannot be
reduced to practical function or made simply a product of construction logic, it is inseparable from these aspects at many
points in its history. Beeby's appraisal is important because
it suggests that ornament did not vanish altogether; rather, it
was subsumed into methodology by being made inseparable
from how an organization was derived. We argue that organizing patterns must be legible to be considered ornament,
and that some of Beeby's examples are thus a stretch in this
regard. Nevertheless, his description of the method is very
much in line with current approaches to the production of
ornament via pattern-making, whereby ornament is used to
construct surfaces and forms, rather than being something
that is applied to them.[29] From this perspective, the modernists who opposed ornament were incorrect to assume that
predetermined styles alone contributed to its creation. In fact,
Art Nouveau, a movement from which much contemporary
ornament in architecture draws inspiration, was a purposeful
rejection of historicism.

      Proponents of Art Nouveau attempted to show that
style, as defined through ornament, should be based not
on tropes drawn from classical and medieval styles, but on
interpretations of nature.[30] The fluid lines and dynamic patterns seen in Art Nouveau were inspired, in no small part, by
developments in the understanding of natural phenomena that
occurred in the nineteenth century, including Charles Darwin's
On the Origin of Species (1859), Ernst Haeckel's *Challenger
Monograph* (1887) and *Art Forms in Nature* (1899), both of which
drew heavily on Darwin's thought, and D'Arcy Thompson's
On Growth and Form (1917). Art Nouveau designers and artists were deeply influenced by the implication of evolutionary
theory and mutation, as well as inspired by the idea that

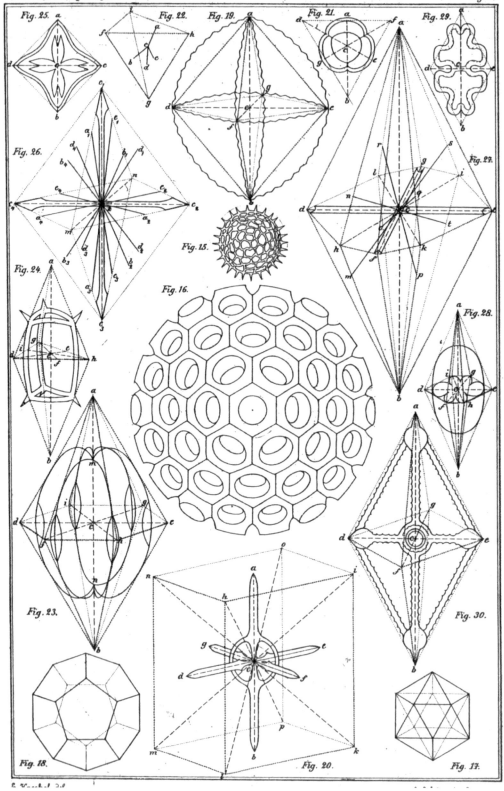

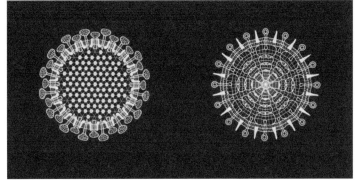

nature had a vitalism that came from within; it was an art of metamorphosis. Haeckel, who coined the term *ecology* in 1866, used ornamental styles to present his scientific discoveries, though some criticized him for misrepresenting life forms. He illustrated individually perfected symmetrical structures and arranged multiple organisms within each drawing using bilateral symmetry.[31] Others have more recently argued that his use of ornamental stylings made the unfamiliar seem familiar: "The foreign forms that he demonstrated—filtered through decorative lenses—were no longer foreign to his contemporaries, who were able to assimilate them."[32] This notion of style as a means of conveying information—or to make one sympathetic to the reception of this information—is critically important to our reading of contemporary landscape projects that utilize ornamental configurations to display landscape processes. Even for a scientist like Haeckel, artistic intuition and interpretation were not seen as being in opposition to information or knowledge; rather, his beliefs about evolutionary processes were embedded in his choice of drawing style. As historian of science Martin Kemp demonstrates, the "look" of science is as indicative of cultures and periods as are the styles defined through historical studies of the arts.[33] Every cultural product, whether in science or design, has inherent biases that are prefiltered through specific instruments, modes of visualization, and individuals' stylistic predilections.

Nonetheless, the visual consistency associated with style is often met with suspicion in landscape architecture and seen as being at odds with a careful reading of site and context. The supposed modernist rigor of a site- and program-based design process still carries with it heavy skepticism regarding style and ornament. James Corner, for example states, "An effective design is always an original response, so much that a project isn't really about a design, or a style, or a look; it's about a unique, highly customized reaction to found conditions."[34] Similarly, a principal at Michael Van Valkenburgh Associates rejects the notion of style as a compositional device:

11. Ernst Haeckel. Plate depicting the underlying polygonal and circular geometries found in natural forms. Originally published in *Generelle Morphologie der Organismen*, v. 1 (1866).

12. Various diatom species captured through photomicrography, 2016. The ornamental arrangement of the algae was created by scientists and harkens back to the drawings of Ernst Haeckel.

13. Laura Splan, *Doilies*, 2004, computerized machine embroidered lace, 16.75" x 16.75".
Unlike the motifs of traditional lace doilies, these computerized doilies reveal the patterns of microscopic viruses. SARS and Influenza are represented here.

Ornamental Patterns

16" bloom   14.4" bloom   12.8" bloom   11.2" bloom   9.6" bloom   8" bloom

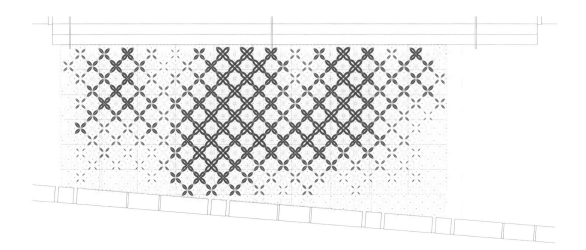

How the park looks as an overall composition doesn't matter much to Van Valkenburgh. Its order arises instead from the efforts of its designers to realize the distinctive potentials of its many parts in resistance to "the tyranny of an overriding style."[35]

This position presumes that the imposition of an overall order, the appearance of consistency in a site, or even consistency among multiple projects by the same designer (i.e., the designer's distinctive "signature") runs counter to the careful and thoughtful reading of a site—a sentiment reminiscent of that expressed by the landscape modernists quoted earlier.[36] However, if style is, at its simplest level, defined as the principles according to which something is designed, then there are no style-less landscapes. The antipathy to style is usually just an aversion to someone else's style, or perhaps a distaste for stylistic overtness, the latter of which ornament is fantastically guilty.

Ornament is meant to be seen and comprehended, which implies that it carries a "message." At present, this communicative dimension of ornament is dismissed on the grounds that forms and styles are undecodable, especially given the plethora of signs arising from today's mass communications. Many may argue that buildings and landscapes cannot communicate through traditional symbolic means but can only produce sensations; yet the evocation of wildness or naturalism, for example, which may or may not be more ecologically or socially functional than more ordered or regular forms, is

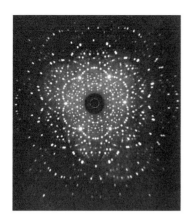

itself an intentional stylistic choice that carries symbolic value regarding one's attitude about humans' relationship to nature. This is not to say that experience alone can produce effects that are directly translatable into ethical or didactic dimensions; on the contrary, no linear cause-and-effect link between experience and knowledge is possible, as many other factors determine their relationship, including culturally learned preferences.[37] Communication as defined here, however, does not correspond to specific meanings or knowledge, but it does trust in the capacity of design to structure experiences and to make relationships legible. Style, then, with its more or less unified ensemble, can be understood as a mode of comprehending and expressing relationships between the material order and communicative order of a landscape.[38] Though ornament is often conflated with the visual (i.e., the superficial), architect Lars Spuybroek is correct to emphasize that "looking" is not static; rather, aesthetic relations happen in real time and space, and it is the *activity* of pattern recognition—not the resultant order—that enables empathy between a person and the object or environment that they observe or inhabit.[39] In this way, ornament acts as a framing device and can be used to heighten awareness of landscape processes.

Resemblances Versus Rules

> The history of the discourse and practices
> of ornamentation has been constant witness to
> the debates on how the ornamental should
> relate to the natural—whether ornaments should
> faithfully represent the wondrous creations
> of nature ipso facto or if a more humble response
> to the incredible beauty and sophistication
> of natural things could be arrived at by simply
> abstracting them.[40]
> —Gunalan Nadarajan

14. PEG office of landscape + architecture, *Dew Point*, Philadelphia, 2010.
The overlapping circle geometry (top) was used as an underlying organization to create a gradient of floral figures that transition from isolated flowers to a patterned field.

15. X-Ray crystallography of the mineral beryl.

The interpretation of nature in ornamental forms often falls into two broad though not mutually exclusive categories.

As described in the above quote, the first approach involves the representation of an organism's form or structure, as in Haeckel's drawings, the botanic motifs found in much Art Nouveau work, or contemporary work by Hernan Diaz Alonso, Greg Lynn, Florencia Pita, and others. The second interpretation is less mimetic because nature is abstracted into mathematical and rule-based forms; thus geometric lines and shapes are manipulated to create patterns through rotation, mirroring, and packing or nesting of shapes that in turn create secondary and tertiary figures, such as stars or flowers. This latter approach can be seen across many eras and cultures, and the practice was lauded by Owen Jones in his highly influential book *The Grammar of Ornament* (1856).[41] Jones believed that ornament should interpret the laws of nature via geometric abstraction and pattern rather than mimic nature's external appearance. He declared that ornamentation based on *rules* rather than *resemblances* was superior owing to its flexibility as a method; this stance would allow for a continuous reinvention of ornamental forms and enable designers to challenge the eclecticism that characterized the architecture and design of his day.[42] As with Beeby's interpretation of modern architecture, the importance of Jones's reading is that the interaction between ornament and the object with which it is affiliated is structured through patterns and formal relationships rather than through symbols or icons alone.[43] In such an approach, ornament and pattern are inseparable. Below, we describe projects that use this method of pattern-making with abstracted geometries (rules) as well as highlight projects that use more representational forms (resemblances) to derive their organizations.

Within landscape architecture, the use of symbols is celebrated in some instances, especially when their associations are more abstract, as in Burle Marx's wavy paving patterns along the beach in Copacabana. At other times, the use of symbols is disparaged as overt branding, such as West 8's proposal to construct wetlands framed by boardwalks in the shape of the maple leaf (which appears on Canada's flag) for Toronto's waterfront. The design has been criticized as

Dynamic Patterns: Visualizing Landscapes in a Digital Age

"too easy," as something akin to a joke, and, more seriously, as colonialistic.[44] Here, the maple leaf serves first and foremost as a national symbol rather than as an index of water filtering processes, and the maple leaf as symbol has no direct or indirect association with water. It is, however, used as a framing device, which is a role that ornament has long served.[45] In other instances, West 8's use of icons has ranged from surface materials, such as the large graphic floral paving in *Madrid Rio*, to forms of spatial organization that rely on the repetition of floral motifs to make a series of inhabitable parterres or topography. Examples of the latter approach include the parterre at Santa Giulia, Milan, and the site organization, building, and landforms at Governors Island, New York. Whether as surface appliqué or spatial elaboration, West 8's designs are a contemporary evocation of traditional ornament, in that they are drawn from botanical motifs and are recognizable as such. This approach is also seen in Mecanoo's *Aberdeen City Gardens* proposal, which is reminiscent of Art Nouveau, albeit supersized to the scale of a park. These examples use recognizable icons as they have been conventionalized through the history of ornamentation. The choice of ornamental motif is arbitrary, in the sense that there is no attempt to relate its symbolism to its function in any way; the designers simply use repetition to systematize a set of simple figures to create spatial structure.[46]

Other recent examples manifest an attempt by the designer to create a close association between the representational aspects of the work — how nature is interpreted as ornamental through geometry, icons, or symbols — and the functionality of the landscape to which the ornament refers. As we observed earlier, history shows the common belief that ornament is completely detached from function to be inaccurate. In buildings, for example, nonfunctional elements can be expressive of the structure or underlying construction to which they are affixed, even if the ornament itself does not fulfill any structural function (such as by supporting a physical load). In other words, ornament is used to intensify the aesthetic effect of a form or structure.[47] In landscape architecture, one aspect of function that has become prevalent today

16. Roberto Burle Marx, *Flamengo Park*, Rio de Janeiro, 1959–63.
Burle Marx created a variety of iconic public landscapes using a diversity of topographic and material patterns. This surface was made with two cultivars of St. Augustine grass.

17. Roberto Burle Marx, *Copacabana Beach* promenade, 1969–72, inspired by traditional Portuguese paving.

Ornamental Patterns

18. West 8, Competition entry for *Toronto Central Waterfront*, 2006.

19. West 8, *Avenida de Portugal*, Madrid Rio, 2006–11.

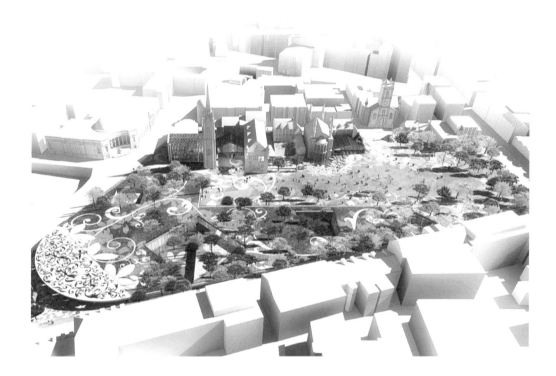

20. West 8, *River Garden* at Toledo Bridge, Madrid Rio, 2006–11.

21. Mecanoo, *Aberdeen City Gardens*, 2011. The continuous figuration of the floral motif organizes landscape, building, circulation, and activities. The motif's varied scale, height, and material creates a functionally diverse yet aesthetically coherent organization.

is the creation of habitat as infrastructure. Such ecological infrastructures are created in response to rising tides, storm surges, and stormwater management. This aspect of landscape function is ripe for articulation.

The repetition of figures can conjoin functional value with a high degree of legibility. Two unbuilt projects serve as examples of this approach. Fabrizio Matillana's *Marsh Condenser*, inspired by the structure of a nautilus shell, collects sediment in order to restore lost marshland. Matillana describes his "eco-machine" as an "evolutionary infrastructure."[48] After modeling the fluid dynamics of a portion of the estuary, he proposed locating a series of spiraling "shells" oriented to maximize sediment capture that would enable vegetation to take root. Similarly, Yongjun Jo and Kyung-Kuhn Lee's *Horizontal Dike* for Miami, Florida, is a two-part structure in which Y-shaped and tripod frames provide the support for palm-fiber mats fastened to them. The frame structure was inspired by the root structure of mangroves, and the designers propose that its position be fixed in vertical, diagonal, and horizontal configurations. Through collecting sediment and allowing actual mangroves to take root, they envision the dike evolving into a thick mat that offers protection from inundation during storm surges. As sea levels rise, the surface area of the dike would continue to thicken and rise as the mangroves and sediment expand their territory. Both projects *evoke* nature through their representational forms, and they also *invoke* nature because they are designed to induce physical change in the environment resulting in habitat creation through the colonization of soil, plants, and animals.

The development of *Marsh Condenser* and *Horizontal Dike* was greatly aided by computer flow models and parametric software. For both schemes, hydrological modeling determined the extent of the projects. Instead of defining the site by a bounded condition, such as property lines or drawing a dividing line between water and land as it is often demarcated on maps, the sites of intervention were defined by patterns represented as gradients of flow direction and intensity. These gradients are the same as the accretive patterns

Dynamic Patterns: Visualizing Landscapes in a Digital Age

22. Fabrizio Matillana, *Marsh Condenser*, 2008, physical model.

23. *Marsh Condenser*. Drawing of spiral composed with Y-shaped units.

described in chapter 1 and were made possible through the use of digital models. Though the resulting patterns (gradients) cannot be divided into modules, unlike line- or shape-based ornamentation in which each part is aggregated to create the whole ensemble, every force or point within the field is related to its adjacent condition. In the second part of the design process, when the structural elements of the nautilus and mangrove were determined, digital models were not essential; however, the structures' aggregation into patterns was greatly facilitated by parametric software and indeed would have been difficult to achieve otherwise. Parametric tools facilitate the manipulation of geometries in novel ways, giving contemporary expression to the notion of ornament as the home of metamorphosis, where forms evoke energy flowing through matter.[49]

Many scholars have noted the patterned and field-like qualities of contemporary ornament. For example, Picon notes that today's geometries, comprised of labyrinthine modules, connections, and processes, perform more as permeable membranes than as masks.[50] Similarly, architectural historian Vittoria Di Palma states that the "all-over, integrated ornamental surface of today's architecture is analogous to other contemporary mergings of figure and ground, object and field," and Spuybroek states that patterns are "true expressions of formation as time-dependent; the spatial forms [that result] are only the final products of such periodicity."[51] Spuybroek also explains that ornament needs to be composed with flexible figures of which there are many, that these many figures must *configure*, addressing design issues as they do so, and, finally, that, through configuring, they must enter the material domain.[52]

   Marsh Condenser and *Horizontal Dike* exemplify these characteristics of interwoven and enmeshed "thick surfaces" that undergo change, both in the initial deployment of their structures by means of geometrical transformation and in how the projects are designed to adapt over time. The link between the forms (sea life interpreted as either nautilus shell or mangrove) and their functions (sediment collection and plant growth) are closely allied because, in each case, the form is chosen for its symbolic value *and* its utility. The designers do not default to engineering conventions to provide solutions to the problem of shoreline reconstruction, which is an agenda at the forefront of our field; instead, they use ornamental patterns to heighten the appearance and, therefore, the awareness and cultural relevance of these functions. Contrary to the criticism that ornament cannot be site-specific, these projects, if built, would be materially embedded within their respective sites. Their forms are simultaneously applied and emergent, representational and indexical. In these examples, ornamental patterns are both an underlying geometric order to which nature is reduced as well as a physical system into which nature expands.[53]

24. Yongjun Jo and Kyung-Kuhn Lee, *Horizontal Dike*, Miami, 2011. Drawing of Y-shaped frame and palm-fiber mat.

25. Bird's eye view of Watson Island.

Dynamic Patterns: Visualizing Landscapes in a Digital Age

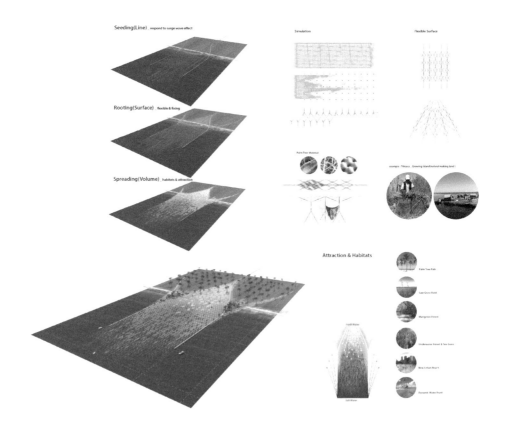

Seeding(Line) _ respond to surge wave effect

Rooting(Surface) _ flexible & fixing

Spreading(Volume) _ habitats & attraction

Simulation

Flexible Surface

Palm Tree Moment

example : Tribute _ Growing island/natural making land !

Attraction & Habitats

Palm Tree Park

Low Grass Field

Mangrove Forest

Underwater Forest & Sea Grass

New Urban Beach

Dynamic Water Front

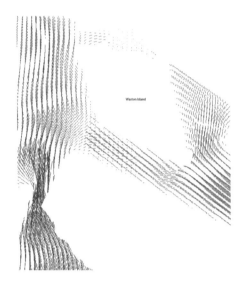

Washon Island

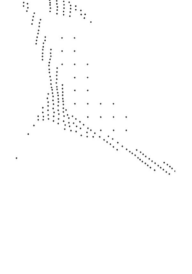

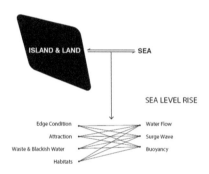

ISLAND & LAND ⟷ SEA

SEA LEVEL RISE

Edge Condition — Water Flow
Attraction — Surge Wave
Waste & Blackish Water — Buoyancy
Habitats

26. *Horizontal Dike.* Water simulation
and geometric framework for locating
the mangrove-inspired structures.

Walking Root System
- From the water edge, the root walk to the sea and inland

Program
-Making new attraction by hybriding the existing stucture and program

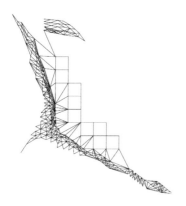

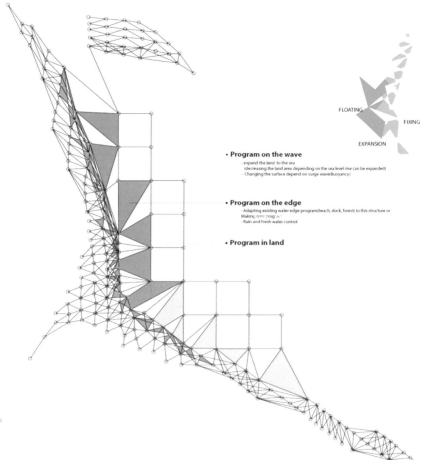

FLOATING

FIXING

EXPANSION

• **Program on the wave**
- expand the land to the sea
(decreasing the land area depending on the sea level rise can be expanded)
- Changing the surface depend on surge wave(Buoyancy)

• **Program on the edge**
- Adapting existing water edge program(beach, dock, forest) to this structure or
Making new program
- Rain and Fresh water control

• **Program in land**

The next two examples are not located in areas subject to the continual flux and quick succession of physical changes that occur in marshlands or bays. However, they are similar to the previous pair of projects in that the designers use repetition to systematize their organization of the landscape. Toyo Ito's proposal for *Parque de la Gavia* in Madrid, which was only partially built, uses a repeating icon to express on-site water cleansing and distribution. This project did not depend on parametric models for its organization, but it shows the same ambition as *Marsh Condenser* and *Horizontal Dike* in its use of ornamental forms to make a landscape system legible. Ito's team designed a module that is emblematic of the fractal structure of a branching tree — dendritic like many water flow patterns. The designers then repeated the module ten times across the site's highest elevations to form a water filtration system. Four of the figures were designed to receive water directly from a sewage treatment plant, and the other six figures receive water from the first four. The module does not aggregate to create a connected field, as in *Horizontal Dike*, and it is more abstract than the nautiluses of the *Marsh Condenser*. As in these other projects, however, repetition creates a correlation among the figures while also allowing differences among them for both functional and experiential purposes. The project conjoins spatial and material qualities with the environmental mandates now required of landscapes, many of which concern water collection and cleansing. The figures are not marginal or separate elements within the purview of civil engineering; on the contrary, they are the primary structure by which the site's topography and planting are organized.

In *Complementary Contradiction,* a hypothetical proposal for a cleared and leveled 61-acre site in downtown Las Vegas, Joe Kubik used repetition to showcase contrasting vegetation patterns. He proposed creating microclimates derived from solar orientation and from moisture levels, based on topography and proximity to groundwater. He utilized a repeating arabesque figure, inspired by the Fibonacci structure found in many desert plants, to form an undulating

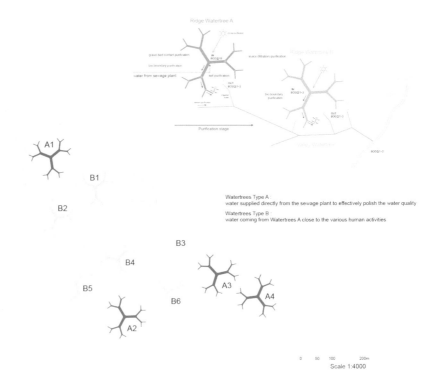

Ridge Watertree A

gravel bed contact purification

bio boundary purification

water from sewage plant

Ridge Watertree B

sluice (filtration) purification

soil purification

bio boundary purification

Purification stage

A1

B1

B2

Watertrees Type A :
water supplied directly from the sewage plant to effectively polish the water quality

Watertrees Type B :
water coming from Watertrees A close to the various human activities

B3

B4

A3

B5

B6

A4

A2

0   50   100   200m

Scale 1:4000

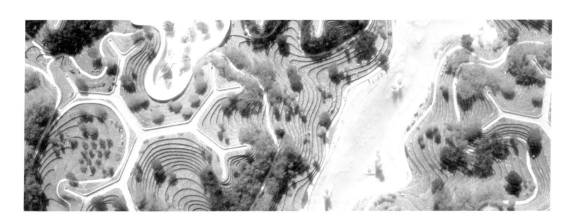

27. Toyo Ito, *Parque de la Gavia*, Madrid, 2003. Site plan showing water filtration system.

28. *Parque de la Gavia*. Model showing the grading in relation to the water filtration modules. Each module was intended to have different materials, edge profiles, aeration features, flow characteristics, and planting in order to diversify the experiences when interacting with water.

29. Joe Kubik, *Complementary Contradiction*, Las Vegas, 2009, bird's eye view of site.

30. *Complementary Contradiction.* Milled model of topography.

topography and path structure. The arabesques mark the distinction between the flatness of the site's edges and its sloping interior. The interior contains a gradient of small mounds and depressions that display red-blooming desert vegetation grouped according to bloom time and microclimate. This approach conjoins the iconic arabesque found in many ornamental traditions with gradients, a more contemporary type of pattern. Additionally, a third pattern of multiple arabesques is distributed across the site to create a spectacle of solar-powered lights.

Complementary Contradiction addresses drought, aridity, and energy sources, but does so through ornamental displays, linking surface with substance. It is impossible to separate its function and its style. The arabesque landscape figures and solar flares are boldly ornamental, consistent with the way in which Las Vegas has been constructed as a tourist attraction, yet they frame a more delicate environment that corresponds to the broader environmental context in which the city is situated. The project utilizes botanic motifs to display botanic zones; moreover, it fuses the representational and the real, the applied and the indexical (through the registration of water levels), the local spectacle and the regional extremes of arid and wet.[54]

Conclusion: Framing Function

Throughout its history, ornament has been associated with pleasure, allure, and the ability to "ignite the imagination."[55] Ornamental patterns, more so than any other patterns, are intended to entice and delight. This has made them susceptible to dismissal on the grounds that these qualities are excessive. There is simply more important work to be done, so the argument goes. For this reason, some wish to protect ornament by foregrounding its utility. Although we have explained the projects in this chapter, in part, through their functional criteria, this is not to say that they are valid because of their utility; it is simply the case that certain functions are expected or required of landscapes and that we should engage them with more imagination than standardization permits.

The projects highlighted in this chapter demonstrate how ornament can be reconceived in today's environmental contexts. They are not reduced to quantifiable solutions to a problem, nor are they restorations in any strict sense. They are inspired by forms found in nature but do not appear natural; that is, they neither mimic landscapes that we would assume to be or recognize as natural, nor do they replicate earlier representations of nature, such as we find in nineteenth-century parks. They are, nevertheless, site- and context-specific, as long as context is understood in broad and inescapably multiple ways. Encouraging an ecological ethos or a "consciousness of milieu" entails responding to endemic conditions, which include imported palm trees and mangroves in Miami or the arabesque of a Fibonacci spiral and the arid desert vegetation in Las Vegas.[56] As the quantifiable functions of landscape have become more central, especially with regard to the design of "green" infrastructure, equal attention must be given to the historical, cultural, and experiential dimensions of our changing relationship to nature and how these ideas are manifest in designed landscapes. The range of expressions that we see today indicates that ornament remains a topic of interest and holds continuing relevance as an element that serves these social and cultural functions.[57]

31. *Complementary Contradiction*.
Perspective view of the topographic
low point where the surface nears
groundwater.

Afterword

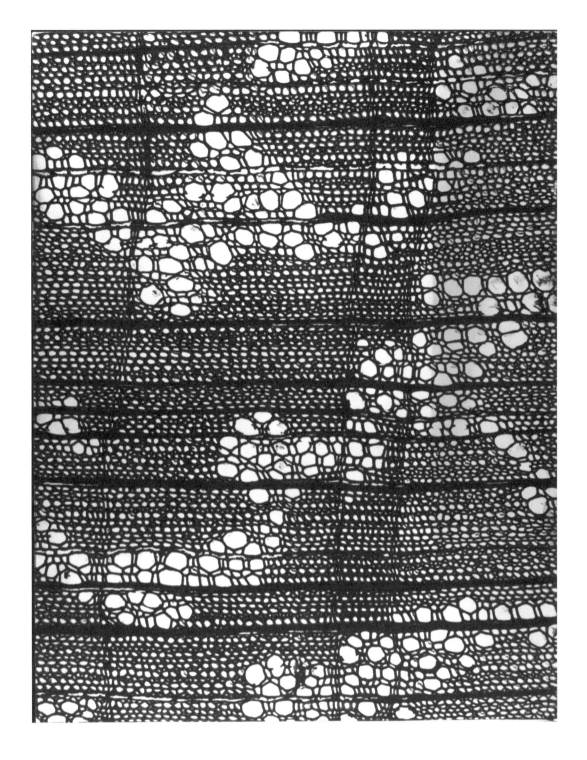

György Kepes, *Transverse section of Osmanthus wood: 50X*, 1951, photographic enlargement on particleboard.

The display of and engagement with processes has been inherent in the making of landscapes throughout history. The many manifestations of this process-orientated engagement reveal how we perceive our affiliation with nature at a given point in time. As argued throughout this book, patterns represent one way to render this relationship comprehensible. The approaches described—topological, behavioral, and ornamental—each prioritize a different aspect of a project's formation, a different kind of pattern-finding or pattern-forming, that relates both to design methods and to material processes in the landscape itself.

New techniques and modes of visualization have the potential to change how we "see." For centuries, humans have created tools to uncover and understand the complexities that underlie the immediately visible characteristics of our environment. Today, ever more elaborate methods and devices are created to perceive, interpret, and open horizons of insight into our world. This much seems obvious, but the belief persists that the newest forms of digital media are somehow more detached from the real world than earlier forms of media, just as there is widespread skepticism today about patterns and surface in designed landscapes. This book's structure will perhaps intensify some criticisms in this regard. It will invite reproaches similar to those directed at Kepes's work, in particular criticism regarding the comparison of many kinds of patterns based on visual resemblance, which presumably ignores the vast differences among them. As one commentator on Kepes noted, "Substance and scale no longer mattered as long as a common pattern was discernible."[1] We are not, however, arguing for an immutable or universal form of pattern. Nor are we proposing that visually homologous patterns across vast scales are the same. Rather, we are arguing that patterns are inherently relational and that the search for and the creation of patterns are endemic to many scientific and artistic endeavors. In both Kepes's "ecological consciousness" and Bateson's ecological episteme, what is most important is the *process* of knowing, which

Dynamic Patterns: Visualizing Landscapes in a Digital Age

comes through the aesthetic dimension. It is our core argument that pattern, in its many and diverse forms, is a primary way to tap into this aesthetic dimension.

Notes

Preface

1. For example, a recent book that focuses on the role of digital media in the formation and making of landscapes is Jillian Walliss and Heike Rahmann, *Landscape Architecture and Digital Technologies: Re-conceptualising Design and Making* (New York: Routledge, 2016).

2. Many others have written on pattern. The absence of Christopher Alexander's *A Pattern Language* will likely be noted. Though his opus has many insights, and the depth and quantity of his work is exceptional, his search for patterns was a search for universal principles that could produce a "timeless way of building," which is not a goal of ours. See Alexander et al., *A Pattern Language: Towns, Buildings, Construction* (New York: Oxford University Press, 1977).

3. György Kepes, *The New Landscape in Art and Science* (Chicago: Paul Theobald and Co., 1963; first printing 1956), 17.

Introduction

1. György Kepes used the phrase "ecological consciousness" in 1972; see Kepes, ed., *Arts of the Environment* (New York: George Braziller, 1972), 1, 170. See also James Corner, "Ecology and Landscape as Agents of Creativity," in *Ecological Design and Planning*, eds. George F. Thompson and Frederick R. Steiner (New York: John Wiley and Sons, Inc., 1997), 87.

2. The phrase "ecology of mind" refers to Gregory Bateson, *Steps to an Ecology of Mind* (Chicago: University of Chicago Press, 2000).

3. Jon Goodbun states, "Outside of the biological sciences, ecology has come to signify something closer to a paradigm rather than a specific discipline, as a culture and holistic science of systemic interconnection in general." See Goodbun, "Gregory Bateson's Ecological Aesthetics—an Addendum to Urban Political Ecology," *Field* 4, no. 1 (2011): 35.

4. This historical trajectory is compellingly laid out in the recently published collection by Chris Reed and Nina-Marie Lister, eds., *Projective Ecologies* (Actar and Harvard University, 2014). Lister and Reed describe their endeavor as "an explicit recognition of a plurality of ecological theories and applied research underpinning contemporary understandings of cultural and natural living systems" (p. 16). In the same publication, Christopher Hight notes a tendency to stretch ecology to suit any interpretation: "[Ecology] has served as a poetic metaphor, techno-scientific imperative, and aesthetic justification. It has been employed to argue for a return to traditional architecture and used for the most rococo parametricism; [it] has become an accreditation requirement and marketing tool. Thus … as the term proliferates, it is in danger of becoming a shibboleth applied to everything yet meaning almost nothing." See Hight, "Designing Ecologies," in *Projective Ecologies*, eds. Reed and Lister, 85. Similarly, S. T. A. Pickett, M. L. Cadenasso, and J. M. Grove observe, "Any technical term in ecology has three kinds of connotation: meaning, model, and metaphor," and they add, "The emergent metaphorical connotations of the ecosystem concept are many, and often contradictory. Ecosystems are viewed as machines, or organic entities, or cybernetic code." Pickett et al., "Resilient Cities: Meaning, Models, and Metaphor for Integrating the Ecological, Socio-economic, and Planning Realms," *Landscape and Urban Planning* 69 (2004): 370, 372.

5. We use the phrase "systems thinking" throughout the book because it is broader than the systems theories arising out of particular disciplines.

6. Donella H. Meadows in *Thinking in Systems: A Primer*, ed. Diana Wright (White River Junction, VT: Chelsea Green, 2008), 190.

7. Definitions of the relation of pattern to systems are too numerous to cite, since patterns are inherent to systems. These quotations are from David S. Walonick, "General Systems Theory" (1993), accessed March 29, 2015, www.statpac.org/walonick/systems-theory.htm, and Donella H. Meadows, *Thinking in Systems*, 188. Meadows's full observation reads that a system is a "set of elements or parts that is coherently organized and interconnected in a pattern or structure that produces a characteristic set of behaviors, often classified as its 'function' or 'purpose.'" Also, "Systems thinking is about patterns of relationships and how these translate into emergent behaviors," according to James J. Kay, "An Introduction to Systems Thinking," in *The Ecosystem Approach: Complexity, Uncertainty, and Managing for Sustainability*, eds. David Waltner-Toews, James J. Kay, and Nina-Marie E. Lister (New York: Columbia University Press, 2008), 3.

8. Eugene Odum described ecosystems in *Fundamentals of Ecology* (Philadelphia: W. B. Saunders Co., 1953), 9, and Howard T. Odum outlined the energy language that he termed "energese" in *Environment, Power, and Society* (New York, NY: John Wiley & Sons, 1971) and later in *Systems Ecology: An Introduction* (New York: John Wiley & Sons, 1983). The term ecosystem, however, did not take on its close affiliation with energy until the Odums' work in the 1950s.

9. On Bateson's notion of "media ecology," see William Kaizen, "Steps to an Ecology of Communication: Radical Software, Dan Graham, and the Legacy of Gregory Bateson," *Art Journal* 67, no. 3 (Fall 2008): 87.

10. Peter Harries-Jones describes Bateson's concerns about the mechanistic view of ecology by means of a pair of questions: "Would the new science of ecology, in which so many now placed hope, prove any better than its forebears if ecological science still embraced the same framework of thinking about the pre-eminence of the material forces of nature? And what advance in thinking would an unreconstructed materialism bring about in the eco-management of nature?" Harries-Jones, "Understanding Ecological Aesthetics: The Challenge of Bateson," *Cybernetics and Human Knowing* 12, no. 1–2 (2005): 64.

11. Peter Harries-Jones, *A Recursive Vision: Ecological Understanding and Gregory Bateson* (Toronto: University of Toronto Press, 2002; first printing 1995), 6.

12. Controversy continues to rage over whether population growth is as great a problem as was presumed in such publications as Donella H. Meadows et al., *The Limits to Growth* (New York: Universe Books, 1972) and Paul Ehrlich, *The Population Bomb* (New York: Ballantine Books, 1968). Population projections were based on expectations of birth rates that have not been fulfilled. If current birth rates are used, global population will in fact decrease significantly. More controversial is the fact that the focus was on birth rates rather than on consumption rates and resource distribution. The latter measures expose great discrepancies between the populations of wealthy countries and the rest of the world.

13. This view of ecology as encompassing realms far beyond science was further promoted by the philosopher Félix Guattari in 1989. See *The Three Ecologies*, trans. Ian Pindar and Paul Sutton (London: The Athlone Press, 2000), which opens with an epigraph from Bateson.

14. For an excellent essay on the comparative influence of cybernetics in Ian McHarg and Lawrence Halprin, see Margot Lystra, "McHarg's Entropy, Halprin's Chance: Representations of Cybernetic Change in 1960s Landscape Architecture," *Studies in the History of Gardens & Designed Landscapes* 34, no. 1 (2014): 71–84.

15. Lystra makes this point as well: "Most environmental designers did not embrace ecology as conducted by scientists—an experimental, deliberative, often inconclusive endeavor. Rather, with management as their goal, they saw in ecological concepts a means to bring new levels of objectivity and authority into their field. The mantle of science was embraced, not in connection with scientific method, but as a way to support environmental priorities—and as a means for bringing new legitimacy to the landscape architectural profession." Lystra, "McHarg's Entropy, Halprin's Chance," 83.

16. For a recent description of this shift, see Reed and Lister, *Projective Ecologies*. Also see Kristina Hill, "Shifting Sites," in

Site Matters: Design Concepts, Histories, and Strategies, ed. Carol Burns and Andrea Kahn (New York and London: Routledge, 2005), 131–55; Robert E. Cook, "Do Landscapes Learn? Ecology's 'New Paradigm' and Design in Landscape Architecture," in *Environmentalism in Landscape Architecture*, ed. Michel Conan (Washington, DC: Dumbarton Oaks, 2000), 115–32, also reprinted in *Projective Ecologies*, 218–37.

17. See Fritjof Capra, "Systems Theory and the New Paradigm," in *Ecology*, ed. Carolyn Merchant (Atlantic Highlands, NJ: Humanities Press, 1994).

18. In the 1960s and 1970s, physical chemist Ilya Prigogine did pioneering work on self-organizing systems. The phrase is taken from his book *From Being to Becoming: Time and Complexity in the Physical Sciences* (San Francisco, CA: W. H. Freeman, 1980).

19. On emergence in architecture, see Michael Hensel, Achim Menges, and Michael Weinstock, eds., *AD Emergence: Morphogenetic Design Strategies* 24, no. 3 (2004).

20. Nina-Marie E. Lister, "A Systems Approach to Biodiversity Conservation Planning," *Environmental Monitoring and Assessment* 49 (1998): 123.

21. Corner, "Ecology and Landscape as Agents of Creativity," 102.

22. See Julia Czerniak, ed., *Case: Downsview Park Toronto* (Munich: Prestel, Harvard, 2001), 17.

23. See James Corner Field Operations's project entry in Czerniak, *Case: Downsview Park Toronto*, 58.

24. The OMA/Mau *Tree City* scheme misconstrued the role of process in the making of landscape, thereby reinforcing the false dichotomy between form and process. Most mid-sized to large parks are incrementally financed, which means that they take years to build and are subject to changes in political leadership. Owing to this timeline, as well as the public nature of such projects, many people including government officials, local residents, and numerous public and private entities are involved in their formation.

25. Philosopher Cary Wolfe believes that the OMA/Mau team's winning scheme, *Tree City*, is exemplary of systems thinking because its "underspecification … makes it *more* available to the autopoiesis of other systems in ways not precluded

up front, by choices made *now*." Wolfe, *What Is Posthumanism?* (Minneapolis: University of Minnesota Press, 2010), 210. Although the project succeeds brilliantly in presenting a strategy that would leave it extremely open to its environment and would allow other autopoietic systems to occur within or through it, it fails according to the other criteria set out by Wolfe, which refer to its material realization. Wolfe frames *Tree City* in architectural terms, claiming that it is radical because it promotes an art of time rather than an art of space by refusing to imagine a built work in the form of a building. If viewed from within the frame of landscape architecture, which always assumes that buildings come after landscape, the project loses its alleged radicalism. Wolfe's other case study of an exemplary system–environment reframing that denies its status as representation is Diller, Scofidio, and Renfro's *Blur Building*. With regard to this example, we fully agree with him.

26. For an excellent study on the relations between information and significance, see Paul Beynon-Davies, *Significance: Exploring the Nature of Information, Systems and Technology* (Hampshire, UK: Palgrave Macmillan, 2011).

27. For example, Anne Whiston Spirn focuses on aesthetics (see note 43), as does James Corner in his writings from the early to late 1990s. See also Catherine Howett, "Systems, Signs and Sensibilities: Sources for a New Landscape Aesthetic," *Landscape Journal* 6, no. 1 (1987): 1–12.

28. Sylvia Crowe's presidential address to Journal of the Institute of Landscape Architects, November 1957, p. 4, cited by Anne Whiston Spirn, "The Authority of Nature: Conflict, Confusion, and Renewal in Design, Planning, and Ecology," in *Ecology and Design: Frameworks for Learning*, eds. Bart R. Johnson and Kristina Hill (Washington, DC: Island Press, 2002), 36.

29. Lystra, "McHarg's Entropy, Halprin's Chance," 82.

30. Lystra "McHarg's Entropy, Halprin's Chance," 75. The original comment is from Ian L. McHarg, "An Ecological Method for Landscape Architecture," *Landscape Architecture* 57, no. 2 (1967): 105. Also, Elizabeth K. Meyer later noted that Ian McHarg and Peter Walker were emblematic of the split between ecological and spatial approaches to design. On this divide between science and art (though not presented in terms of pattern), see Meyer, "The Post-Earth Day Conundrum:

Translating Environmental Values into Landscape Design," in *Environmentalism in Landscape Architecture*, ed. Michel Conan (Washington, DC: Dumbarton Oaks, 2000), 187–244.

31. György Kepes, *The New Landscape in Art and Science* (Chicago: Paul Theobald and Co., 1963; first printing 1956), 21.

32. Ian McHarg, "Natural Factors in Planning (1997)," in *The Essential Ian McHarg: Writings on Design and Nature*, ed. Frederick R. Steiner (Washington, DC: Island Press, 2006), 118. For an excellent overview of the contradictions in McHarg's work, see Susan Herrington, "The Nature of Ian McHarg's Science," *Landscape Journal* 29, no. 1 (2010): 1–20.

33. The contradiction between McHarg's method and rhetoric, on one hand, and some of his designs on the other can be seen in his unbuilt proposal for Pardisun Park in Tehran (1975), which was intended to represent five major ecosystems across the world. The project would have required great expense and resources to fabricate such mini-ecosystems and was a blatant contradiction of the values he was attempting to support with his methodology and notion of "fitness."

34. Melanie Simo, "Making the Landscape Visible," in *Peter Walker: Experiments in Gesture, Seriality, and Flatness*, ed. Linda L. Jewell (New York: Rizzoli International Publications, Inc., 1990), 10.

35. Marc Treib, "The Content of Landscape Form (The Limits of Formalism)," *Landscape Journal* 20, no. 2 (2001): 124. For an essay on the various criticisms of pattern, including Treib's, see Karen M'Closkey, "Synthetic Patterns: Fabricating Landscapes in the Age of 'Green,'" *Journal of Landscape Architecture* (Spring 2013): 16–27.

36. Treib's examples of works that celebrate ecological processes include those by Hargreaves Associates, George Descombes, and Dieter Kienast.

37. Treib, "Content of Landscape Form," 120.

38. Ibid, 127.

39. Harries-Jones, *A Recursive Vision*, 203.

40. A fairly recent essay by Simon Swaffield refers to pattern as a "paradigm," focusing primarily on characteristic formal types and their morphological changes over time. Thus Swaffield is looking for patterns and commonalties across projects rather than focusing on the use of patterns within individual projects, as we are doing here. For example, Swaffield compares the relationship between water and woodland in seventeenth-century France and eighteenth-century England. See Swaffield, "Tracing Change: Patterns in Landscape Architecture," *AD: Patterns of Architecture* 79, no. 6 (2009): 54–59.

41. Simon Bell, a forester and landscape architect, formulated his book *Landscape: Pattern, Perception and Process* (New York: Routledge, 1999) as a guide for designers and managers. His primary focus is on ecosystem management and restoration. Also see Sylvia Crowe and Mary Mitchell, eds., *The Pattern of Landscape* (Chichester, UK: Packard Publishing, 1988), which provided the impetus for Bell's undertaking.

42. Richard Forman, one of landscape ecology's most prominent theorists, describes his field as "focus[ing] directly on the whole landscape, ecologically explaining its patterns, how it works in terms of flows and movements, and how it changes spatially over time." Importantly, Forman argues for the importance of aesthetics in formulating ecological approaches to design. See R. T. T. Forman, "The Missing Catalyst: Design and Planning with Ecology Roots," in *Ecology and Design: Frameworks for Learning*, eds. Bart R. Johnson and Kristina Hill (Washington, DC: Island Press, 2002), 98.

43. Anne Whiston Spirn, "The Poetics of City and Nature: Towards a New Aesthetic for Urban Design," *Landscape Journal* 7, no. 10 (1988): 112.

44. Spirn, "The Poetics," 112.

45. Ibid, 110.

46. Harries-Jones, *A Recursive Vision*, 64.

47. Bateson, *Steps to an Ecology of Mind*, 132.

48. Hight, "Designing Ecologies," 101.

49. Mary Catherine Bateson, "Foreword," in Bateson, *Steps to an Ecology of Mind*, xiii.

Chapter 1

1. A. L. Loeb, "Structure and Patterns in Science and Art," *Leonardo* 4, no. 4 (Autumn 1971): 340.

2. Pattern recognition has proved useful for identifying and studying the spatiotemporal forces (hydrological flow, plant succession, soil nutrient depletion, population migration, etc.) that define the features of a geographic area. See Dana Tomlin, "Questionnaire: Models as Generative Processes," in *Models: 306090 Books 11*, eds. Emily Abruzzo, Eric Ellingsen, and Jonathan D. Solomon (New York: Princeton Architectural Press, 2007), 234.

3. The term "datascapes" comes from MVRDV's *MetaCity/Data Town* (Rotterdam: MVRDV/010 Publishers, 1999). MVRDV set out to reveal how our collective choices and behaviors mold our constructed environments using data to illustrate the spatial consequences of our consumption and lifestyle choices.

4. Hans Christian von Baeyer states, "Information is the transfer of form from one medium to another. ... Translating a pattern in one medium into the same pattern, expressed differently in another medium is called coding." See von Baeyer, *Information: The New Language of Science* (Cambridge, MA: Harvard University Press, 2004), 25.

5. According to anthropologist Katja Neves-Graca, Bateson's approach to formal properties is based on theories of morphology (i.e., the living, recursive processes of form) rather than on static and fixed notions of structure. Neves-Graca, " 'Aesthetics': Detached Appreciation or Responsiveness to Connection?" (unpublished paper presented at the Concordia University, Department of Sociology and Anthropology, North York, Ontario, November 16, 2005).

6. Stan Allen and Marc McQuade, eds., *Landform Building* (Baden, Germany: Lars Muller Publishers, 2011), 367, 369.

7. For a description of the relevance of morphogenesis and computation in architecture, see Michael Weinstock, "Morphogenesis and the Mathematics of Emergence," in Michael Hensel, Achim Menges, and Michael Weinstock, eds., *AD Emergence: Morphogenetic Design Strategies* 74, no. 3 (May/June 2004): 10–17. Also see Peter Trummer, "Associative Design: From Type to Population," in *Computational Design Thinking*, eds. Achim Menges and Sean Ahlquist (London: Wiley, 2011), 179–97.

8. Gregory Bateson, *Mind and Nature: A Necessary Unity* (New York: E. P. Dutton, 1979), 13.

9. For an expanded critique of the limitations of digital media use in landscape architecture, see Karen M'Closkey, "Structuring Relations: From Montage to Model in Composite Imaging," in *Composite Landscapes: Photomontage and Landscape Architecture*, eds. Charles Waldheim and Andrea Hansen (Boston: Isabella Stewart Gardner Museum; Ostfildern, Germany: Hatje Cantz Verlag, 2014).

10. "Pattern," *Merriam-Webster Online Dictionary*, accessed January 1, 2015, www.merriam-webster.com/dictionary/pattern.

11. "Topology," *Online Etymology Dictionary*, accessed January 1, 2015, http://etymonline.com/index.php?term=-logy&allowed_in_frame=0.

12. H. Graham Flegg, *From Geometry to Topology* (Mineola, NY: Dover Publications, 2001; first printing 1974), 19.

13. Although the term topology was not formalized in mathematics until the middle of the nineteenth century, the idea is originally attributed to Gottfried Leibniz and is associated with the invention of calculus in the mid-seventeenth century.

14. Referring to geometries in which notions such as length are not fixed or fundamental, Manuel De Landa states, "Architects are familiar with at least one of these geometries, projective geometry (as in perspective projections). In this case, the operation of 'projecting' may lengthen or shrink lengths and areas so these cannot be basic notions. In turn, those properties which do remain fixed under projections may not be preserved under yet other forms of geometry, such as differential geometry or topology. The operations allowed in the latter, such as stretching without tearing, and folding without gluing, preserve only a set of very abstract properties invariant." See De Landa, "Deleuze and the Use of the Genetic Algorithm in Architecture," in *Phylogenesis: FOA's Ark*, ed. Foreign Office Architects (Barcelona: Actar, 2004), 528.

15. Both Christophe Girot and Greg Lynn have acknowledged this affinity. See Girot, "The Elegance of Topology," in *Topology: Topical Thoughts on the Contemporary Landscape*, eds. Christophe Girot, Anette Freytag, Albert Kirchengast, and Dunja Richter (Berlin: Jovis Verlag

Notes

GmbH, 2013); Lynn, *Animate Form* (New York: Princeton Architectural Press, 1999), 28–32.

16. See György Kepes, *The New Landscape in Art and Science* (Chicago: Paul Theobald and Co, 1963; first printing 1956), 205.

17. Ibid., 204.

18. Lawrence Halprin, *Cities* (New York: Reinhold Publishing, 1963), 208; Lawrence Halprin, "Motation," *Progressive Architecture* 46 (1965): 126.

19. Hans Jenny, *Cymatics: The Structure and Dynamics of Waves and Vibrations* (Basel, Switzerland: Basilius Presse, 1967), 10.

20. RSVP is an abbreviation for Resources, Scores, Valuaction, and Performance. Halprin likened his scoring method to a computer punch card; see Lawrence Halprin, *The RSVP Cycles: Creative Processes in the Human Environment* (New York: George Braziller, 1973; first printing 1969), 50.

21. Stan Allen, *Practice: Architecture, Technique and Representation* (New York: Routledge, 2003; first printing 2000), 41–42. Allen also says that the "products of notation do not necessarily resemble the notation itself," and he adds, "If architecture is to work beyond the level of image it needs to invent new tools to work more effectively within the immaterial networks and systems that comprise the city in the late twentieth century" (pp. 32, 39–40).

22. Halprin subsequently came to believe that the experience and the interactions with the performance participants were more important than the scoring method. For further explanation of the evolution of his scoring method, see Peter Merrimen, "Architecture/Dance: Choreographing and Inhabiting Spaces with Anna and Lawrence Halprin," *Cultural Geographies* 14, no. 4 (2010): 440.

23. Margot Lystra, "McHarg's Entropy, Halprin's Chance: Representations of Cybernetic Change in 1960s Landscape Architecture," *Studies in the History of Gardens & Designed Landscapes: An International Quarterly* 34, no. 1 (2014): 79.

24. Ching-Yu Chang stated, "The essential quality of a score is that it conveys, guides, or controls the interaction of space, time, rhythm, and sequence. A score records past events, prognosticates the future, and influences the present." Chang, "Workshop: Take Part Process to Collective Creativity," in Ching-Yu Chang, ed., *Process Architecture: Lawrence Halprin* 4 (1978): 34.

25. Lystra, "McHarg's Entropy, Halprin's Chance: Representations of Cybernetic Change in 1960s Landscape Architecture," 81.

26. The collaborators on *Flame Orchard* were Kepes, physicist William Walton, artist Mauricio Bueno, and composer Paul Earls. See György Kepes, ed., *The MIT Years: 1945–1977* (Cambridge: MIT Press, 1978), 15, 67.

27. Jenny, *Cymatics,* 39.

28. See Philip Ball, "Pattern Formation in Nature: Physical Constraints and Self-Organising Characteristics," in Achim Menges, ed., *AD: Material Computation* 216 (March/April 2012): 22–27.

29. Ball, "Pattern Formation in Nature," 23–24.

30. Antoine Picon, *Digital Culture in Architecture: An Introduction for the Design Professions* (Basel, Switzerland: Birkhauser, 2010), 151.

31. Carlos Ferrater Partnership and Borja Ferrater, *Synchronizing Geometry: Landscape, Architecture & Construction/ Ideographic Resources* (Barcelona: Actar, 2006), 20.

32. Kepes, *The New Landscape in Art and Science*, 367.

33. Nicholas de Monchaux, "Local Code: Real Estates," in David Gissen, ed., *AD: Territory* 205 (2010): 88–93.

34. Kepes, *The New Landscape in Art and Science*, 206.

35. Peter Harries-Jones, *A Recursive Vision: Ecological Understanding and Gregory Bateson* (Toronto: University of Toronto Press, 2002; first printing 1995), 63.

Chapter 2

1. Peter Harries-Jones defines the relational aspect of pattern as having "no location in the object observed; instead its existence results from a relationship of comparison or contrast *between* two objects." Harries-Jones, *A Recursive Vision: Ecological Understanding and Gregory Bateson* (Toronto: University of Toronto Press, 2002; first printing 1995), 51.

2. Cary Wolfe, *What Is Posthumanism?* (Minneapolis: University of Minnesota Press, 2010), 205.

3. For example, see James Nisbet, *Ecologies, Environments, and Energy Systems in the Art of the 1960s and 1970s* (Cambridge: MIT Press, 2014); Edward A. Shanken, ed., *Systems* (London: Whitechapel Gallery and Cambridge: MIT Press, 2015); Arindam Dutta, *A Second Modernism: MIT, Architecture, and the "Techno-Social" Movement* (Cambridge: MIT Press, 2015); Anne Collins Goodyear, "György Kepes, Billy Klüver, and American Art of the 1960s: Defining Attitudes Toward Science and Technology," *Science in Context* 17, no. 4 (2004): 611–35.

4. For an overview of literature pertaining to Burnham's systems aesthetics, see Edward A. Shanken, "Reprogramming Systems Aesthetics: A Strategic Historiography," *Digital Arts and Culture* (December 2009): 1–7, accessed April 20, 2016, http://escholarship.org/uc/item/6bv363d4.

5. Caroline Jones notes that artist Hans Haacke, for example, "posited no human subject in the art equation." See Jones, "Artist/System" in Dutta, *A Second Modernism*, 509.

6. The quote is from Dutta's introduction, *A Second Modernism*, 40.

7. Cybernetics is no longer a broadly used term, but it is almost synonymous with systems theory. Some have argued that systems theory focuses on "the *structure* of systems and their models, whereas cybernetics [focuses] more on how systems *function*, that is to say how they control their actions, how they communicate with other systems or with their own components." Principia Cybernetica Web, "What are Cybernetics and Systems Science?" accessed April 20, 2016, http://pespmc1.vub.ac.be/cybswhat.html.

8. Massachusetts Institute of Technology Institute Archives and Special Collections, "Guide to the Papers of Norbert Wiener MC.0022," accessed April 20, 2016, https://libraries.mit.edu/archives/research/collections/collections-mc/mc22.html.

9. Kepes taught visual design in the School of Architecture beginning in 1945. Goodyear, "György Kepes, Billy Klüver, and American Art of the 1960s," 617. His desire in founding CAVS was "to provide a model for the interaction of the arts and sciences for society as a whole." Ibid., 618.

10. In addition to the *Cybernetic Serendipity* and *Software, Information Technology* exhibits, the show *Information* (Museum of Modern Art, New York, 1970) exhibited a broad array of artists. This show did not focus on technology *per se* but was premised on the understanding of information as transmission and interpretation. See Nisbet, *Ecologies, Environments, and Energy Systems*, 160–63.

11. The shift away from medium specificity and "objecthood" characterized systems art as well as the roughly concurrent art practices that were labeled "minimalist" and "conceptual" art. For example, art critics Rosalind Krauss and Lucy Lippard describe, respectively, the shift to a "post-medium condition" and the "dematerialized" art object. It is important to acknowledge that our argument is not directed at another significant aspect of systems, conceptual, and process art—namely, its tendency to challenge the boundaries that constrain art production itself, such as institutions and galleries. For an important work in this vein with respect to systems theory, see Niklas Luhmann, *Art as a Social System*, translated by Eva M. Knodt (Stanford: Stanford University Press, 2000).

12. For a more complete description of this project and the significance of Pask's work, see Usman Haque, "The Architectural Relevance of Gordon Pask," *Architectural Design: 4Dsocial: Interactive Design Environments* 77, no. 4 (2007): 54–61.

13. For more on various pieces shown in the *Cybernetic Serendipity* show, see Marcelyn Gow, "Cybernetic Anything …" in *Softspace: From a Representation of Form to a Simulation of Space*, eds. Sean Lally and Jessica Young (London and New York: Routledge and Rice University, 2007). Gow argues that most pieces had technology on display rather than making the machine secondary to the ambience or interactions it produced. The exception, according to Gow, was the piece titled

"Cybernetic Sculpture" by artist Wen-Ying Tsai in collaboration with engineer/artist Frank Turner.

14. See Rainer Usselmann, "The Dilemma of Media Art: Cybernetic Serendipity at the ICA London," *Leonardo* 36, no. 5 (2003): 389–96. Usselmann argues that media art does not have to be limited to spectacle and should be used critically: "Sensory stimuli that re-translate bits of information back into human bandwidth do not need to dumb down, immerse and pacify the human recipient. Media art can … introduce database politics as the site for critical practice, operating from within an all-encompassing 'information paradigm'" (p. 395).

15. On positivism in the American art scene, see Jones, "Artist/System."

16. For an excellent overview of Pask's work on "underspecified goals" using interactive and conversational machines that could give its users agency, see Haque, "The Architectural Relevance of Gordon Pask." Haque states that Pask's work is "not about designing aesthetic representations of environmental data … or making urban structures more spectacular.…It is about designing tools that people themselves may use to construct—in the widest sense of the word—their environments and as a result build their own sense of agency," (p. 61). For an essay that, by contrast, argues that the project changed toward more control with Pask's involvement, see Stanley Mathews, "The Fun Palace: Cedric Price's Experiment in Architecture and Technology," *Technoetic Arts: A Journal of Speculative Research* 3, no. 2 (2005): 73–91.

17. Jack Burnham, "Introduction," in *Great Western Salt Works: Essays on the Meaning of Post-Formalist Art*, ed. Jack Burnham (New York: George Braziller, 1974), 11. Relatedly, Reinhold Martin notes that Kepes' pattern-seeing "was and is commensurate with the logic of this [military-industrial] complex." Martin, *The Organizational Complex* (Cambridge: MIT Press, 2003), 43. See also Caroline A. Jones, "Systems Symptoms," *Artforum International* 51, no. 1 (2012), accessed April 20, 2016, https://proxy.library.upenn.edu/login?url=http://proxy.library.upenn.edu:2175/docview/1039645785?accountid=14707. Jones notes that Burnham's account of systems is unaccountably obscure, owing partially to his mention of the Rand Corporation's use of systems theory in its 1964 publication "Analysis for Military Decisions." She states that "the obvious entanglement of systems theory with the military-industrial complex was a fatal attribute in the eyes of his largely leftist audience during the Vietnam era."

18. Burnham, "Systems Esthetics," in *Great Western Salt Works*, 17.

19. This quote is from a conversation between Edward Shanken and Jack Burnham about Burnham's *Software* exhibit. See Shanken, "Art in the Information Age," *Leonardo* 35, no. 4 (2002): 434.

20. For an excellent introduction to the potentials and limits that the term "Anthropocene" holds for design, see Etienne Turpin, "Introduction: Who Does the Earth Think It Is, Now?" in *Architecture in the Anthropocene: Encounters Among Design, Deep Time, Science and Philosophy*, ed. Etienne Turpin (Ann Arbor, MI: Open Humanities Press, 2013). For a critique of the term "Anthropocene," see Andreas Malm, "The Anthropocene Myth," *Jacobin*, accessed May 2, 2016, www.jacobinmag.com/2015/03/anthropocene-capitalism-climate-change/. Malm argues that this term lets capitalism off the hook and implicates all humanity rather than the powerful few who are driving such environmental changes. Furthermore, he contends, it naturalizes capital and power by portraying social relations as "the natural properties of the species."

21. The term "Anthropocene" was coined in the late 1980s by biologist Eugene Stroermer but was brought to public attention by atmospheric chemist Paul J. Crutzen in 2000. "Post-humanism" includes a broad constellation of philosophers, such as Donna Haraway, N. Katherine Hayles, and Cary Wolfe. For an excellent overview of species thinking and why understanding humans in terms of our deep history—our history as a species—rather than in terms of recorded history is necessary in order to grasp the crisis posed by climate change, see Dipesh Chakrabarty, "The Climate of History: Four Theses," *Critical Inquiry* 35 (2009): 197–222. Though "agents" and "assemblages" are not new terms, they gained renewed relevance after appearing as key concepts in some philosophers' work. For example, the concept of agents is central to Bruno Latour's writing. On this term in relation to the Anthropocene, see Latour, "Agency at the time of the Anthropocene," *New Literary History* 45 (2014): 1–18. "Assemblages," a concept central to Gilles Deleuze, Félix Guattari, and Manuel De Landa, are heterogeneous entities with emergent properties; they are contingent and specific, and they create unities while still recognizing the heterogeneity of the agents that constitute

them. The term "hyperobjects" comes from Timothy Morton, *Hyperobjects: Philosophy and Ecology after the End of the World* (Minneapolis: University of Minnesota Press, 2013).

22. Bruno Latour's publications on this topic are numerous. For a brief overview of his thinking on the relation between art and science, see "An Aesthetics of Proof: a Conversation between Bruno Latour and Francis Halsall on Art and Inquiry," *Environment and Planning D: Society and Space* 30, no. 6 (2012): 963–70.

23. Timothy Morton, *Ecology without Nature: Rethinking Environmental Aesthetics* (Cambridge, MA: Harvard University Press, 2009), 24.

24. Wolfe, *What Is Posthumanism?* 206.

25. Marshall McLuhan, "The Invisible Environment: The Future of an Erosion," *Perspecta* 11 (1967): 165.

26. Ibid.

27. György Kepes, "The Artist's Role in Environmental Self-Regulation," in *Arts of the Environment*, ed. György Kepes (New York: George Braziller, 1972), 184.

28. Kepes notes, "Our potent tools, both conceptual and physical, contain within themselves an important aspect of new human perspectives. The more power-ful the devices we develop through our scientific technology, the more we are interconnected with each other, with our machines, with our environment, and with our own inner capacities." Ibid., 7.

29. György Kepes, ed., *The New Landscape in Art and Science* (Chicago: Paul Theobald and Co., 1963; first printing 1956), 104.

30. Of course, technological advances can be used to argue for further attempts to "control" nature, but this is pure hubris. For example, some geo-engineers support the creation of an atmospheric shield of sulfate particles to reflect the sun's heat. This purported solution to global warming would do nothing to change the causes of the problem and would undoubtedly have other consequences that we cannot foresee. Scientific American, "Geoengineering Is Not a Solution to Climate Change," accessed June 14, 2015, www.scientificamerican. com/article/geoengineering-is-not-a-solu-tion-to-climate-change/.

31. Regarding CAVS, Goodyear states, "Based on the conviction that visual language represented a bridge between art and science, the Center put into prac-tice the Bauhaus and constructivist ide-als Kepes had embraced since the begin-ning of his career." Goodyear, "György Kepes, Billy Klüver, and American Art of the 1960s," 616–17. Reinhold Martin states that for McLuhan "pattern recognition is a process comparable to that of acquiring a new mother tongue, a linguistic home that gives shelter to the human subject awash in a delirious, multimedia envi-ronment, by training him or her to 'see' the hidden, regulating patterns—the grammar, but also the software, if you like—that was running the new machines that were running the new environments, in a recurrent feedback loop." Martin "Environment, c. 1973," *Grey Room* 14 (2004): 89.

32. The energy conservation goals are laudable, but there are troubling aspects to this narrative, especially in areas where entirely new cities are being built on greenfield sites, such as in India and Africa. Corporate-run cities are creating privatized, gated "communities" on a massive scale.

33. In a recent article, architect Rem Koolhaas warns that digital sensor cul-ture means an endless repetition and reinforcement of routine and is always marketed as something that improves our lives rather than in terms of what might be taken away. See Rem Koolhaas, "The Smart Landscape: Intelligent Architecture," *ArtForum* (April 2015), accessed April 19, 2015, https://artforum. com/inprint/issue=201504&id=50735. This warning is not confined to digital technologies but applies to the concept of technology in general. Leo Marx notes that the concept is so vague and abstract that it takes on a life of its own: "The popularity of the belief that tech-nology is the primary force shaping the post-modern world is a measure of our growing reliance on instrumental stan-dards of judgment, and our corresponding neglect of moral and political standards, in making decisive choices about the direction of society. To expose this hazard is a vital task for the human sciences." Marx, " 'Technology': The Emergence of a Hazardous Concept," *Social Research* 64, no. 3 (1997): 984.

34. The phrase "matters of concern" was used by Bruno Latour, "Why Has Critique Run Out of Steam? From Matters of Fact to Matters of Concern," *Critical Inquiry* 30, no. 2 (2004): 225–48.

35. Los Angeles Department of Water and Power, *Owens Lake Habitat Management*

Plan (March 2010), accessed July 18, 2015, http://inyo-monowater.org/wp-content/uploads/2011/09/HabitatMgmtPlan_OwensDryLake_LADWP.pdf.

36. Audubon California, "New Opportunities for Birds at Owens Lake," accessed July 18, 2015, http://ca.audubon.org/conservation/new-opportunities-birds-owens-lake.

37. The birds that inhabit the lake bed are protected by the North American Migratory Bird Treaty Act. For a description of the detrimental effects on the birds, including toxic levels of sodium and metals, see Karen Piper, "Dreams, Dust and Birds: The Trashing of Owens Lake," *Places* (2011), accessed July 18, 2015, https://placesjournal.org/article/dreams-dust-and-birds-the-trashing-of-owens-lake/.

38. Antoine Picon maintains that the turn toward instigating behaviors signifies "the shift from an aesthetics of contemplation to an aesthetics of active participation that lies at the core of the performalist turn within contemporary architecture." Picon, "What Has Happened to Territory?" in David Gissen, ed. *AD Territory: Architecture Beyond Environment* 80, no. 3 (2010): 99.

39. Kepes, *The New Landscape in Art and Science*, 227.

40. McLuhan, "The Invisible Environment," 165.

41. Morton, *Hyperobjects*, 1.

42. Timothy Morton, "Hyperobjects and the End of Common Sense," *Contemporary Condition* (March 18, 2010), accessed July 1, 2015, http://contemporarycondition.blogspot.com/2010/03/hyperobjects-and-end-of-common-sense.html.

43. As Ursula K. Heise writes: "Rapidly increasing data inventories and new digital tools have contributed to this rising interest in large-scale processes and big-picture patterns, as have shifting geopolitical configurations and global ecological crises." See Heise, "Ursula K. Heise Reviews Timothy Morton's Hyperobjects," *Critical Inquiry* (June 4, 2014), accessed May 31, 2015, http://criticalinquiry.uchicago.edu/ursula_k._heise_reviews_timothy_morton.

44. Piezoelectricity is the capacity of materials to generate an electrical charge when they are subjected to a mechanical force. For the *Wave Garden* project, the membranes would produce electrical current from the force of the ocean's waves.

45. See "Wave Garden by Yusuke Obuchi," *Pruned* (June 18, 2005), accessed March 25, 2013, http://pruned.blogspot.com/2005/06/wave-garden-by-yusuke-obuchi.html.

46. Political scientist Jane Bennett describes the electric power grid as an assemblage that has agency in a multitude of ways, none of which can be untangled. Bennett uses the example of the 2003 blackout, which left millions without power in the midwestern and northeastern United States and southern Ontario, Canada, as an example of human-non-human assemblage. A few dispersed outages triggered a cascading effect and massive shutdown, yet it is unknown how or why the system stopped itself. Bennett argues that "agency, conceived now as something distributed along a continuum, extrudes from multiple sites or many loci—from a quirky electron flow and a spontaneous fire to members of Congress who have a neoliberal faith in market self-regulations." Bennett, *Vibrant Matter* (Durham, NC: Duke University Press, 2010), 28.

47. Obuchi asks: "What's the relationship between information and architecture, how you materialize information [*sic*]. This process will radically change the way in which we understand materials, how to manage materials, how to use material in different ways so we can actually generate highly intelligent environments." "Wave Garden: Yusuke Obuchi Interviewed by Chrysostomos Tsimourdagkas," *Floater* (n.d.), accessed March 25, 2013, www.floatermagazine.com/issue01/pdfs/Wave_Garden.pdf.

48. Shanken, in "Art in the Information Age," 436, observes that "meaning and value are not embedded in objects, institutions, or individuals so much as they are abstracted in the production, manipulation and distribution of signs and information."

49. Jon Goodbun, "Gregory Bateson's Ecological Aesthetics: An Addendum to Urban Political Ecology," *Field* 4, no. 1 (2010): 41.

50. For a partial transcript of the event at which Bateson spoke, see Douglas MacAgy, ed., "The Western Round Table on Modern Art (1949)," accessed January 7, 2016, www.ubu.com/historical/wrtma/culture05.htm. Also see Goodbun, "Gregory Bateson's Ecological Aesthetics," 41.

51. Kepes, *Arts of the Environment*, 9.

52. See Adam Curtis's BBC series *All Watched Over by Machines of Loving Grace* (2011), which argues that "What made the systems idea so powerful was that it seemed not to be based on political ideology; it was a scientific idea of organization that mirrored the natural world." The quote is from Part 2, "The Use and Abuse of Vegetational Concepts." www.dailymotion.com/video/x2eagvn_all-watched-over-by-machines-of-loving-grace-2-3-the-use-and-abuse-of-vegetational-concepts-2011_auto (at 43:40).

53. Though we cite Gregory Bateson as a key figure, others were involved in challenging the early and limited interpretation of cybernetics, including anthropologist Margaret Mead, who was seminal in broadening systems thinking. Two distinct interpretations of systems in ecological thought are described by James Nisbet: "The entry of energy systems into ecological thought … unfolded largely along two tracks laid out by the mathematical rigor of Norbert Wiener's cybernetics and the descriptive metaphor of biologist Ludwig von Bertalanffy's general systems theory." Nisbet adds that "artists and critics of the 1960s would continue to work through the perceived difference between biology and technology as the competing scaffolding for understanding ecosystems." Nisbet, *Ecologies, Environments, and Energy*, 6–7.

54. Exhibitions include *Open Systems: Rethinking Art c. 1970* (Tate Modern, 2005) and *Systems Art: Symposium* (Whitechapel Gallery, 2007). Numerous historical and contemporary essays on systems art can be found in Shanken, *Systems*; see also Nisbet, *Ecologies, Environments, and Energy*. Regarding the influence of systems and ecology on artists in the 1960s and 1970s, Nisbet states that their insights remain relevant in terms of how "we continue to negotiate the role of new technologies within the thoroughly hybrid environments of the twenty-first century" (p. 64).

55. See note 17.

56. For a similar argument on the use of hydrodynamic computer simulations, see Eduardo Rico and Enriqueta Llabres Valls, "Interacting with Simulations," in Karen M'Closkey and Keith VanDerSys, eds. *LA + SIMULATION* 4 (2016). Rico and Valls argue that designers should not simply use these tools as data sources to substantiate "technically sound proposals backed up by scientific evidence," but to use them critically and heuristically:

"The designer's task is to derive alternative regimes of effect (using the same abstractions that substantiate these tools) in order to seek new forms of spatial production and to constantly assess them against the existing discourses of territorial disciplines" (p. 60).

57. Jack Burnham notes, "In a systems context, invisibility, or invisible parts, share equal importance with things seen." Burnham, *Great Western Salt Works*, 22.

58. On Bateson's work in relation to the idea of media ecology, see William Kaizen, "Steps to an Ecology of Communication: Radical Software, Dan Graham, and the Legacy of Gregory Bateson," *Art Journal* 67, No. 3 (2008). This essay examines the reception of Bateson's thought as it was developed in the media magazine *Radical Software* in the 1970s.

Chapter 3

1. For example, Antoine Picon states, "Without reinventing Postmodernism, it may be useful to rediscover some of the issues that it raised, beginning with the quest for a renewed legibility of architecture," and "At a more fundamental level than cultural and regional connotations, the new regime of relations between the subject and his/her environment could constitute a major source of symbolic inspiration." Picon, *Ornament: The Politics of Architecture and Subjectivity* (Chichester: John Wiley and Sons, 2013), 145, 152.

2. According to Gülru Necipoğlu and Alina Payne, "Ontological and psychological binaries [have] frequently structured thinking about ornament: ornament versus structure, surface versus plastic form, decadence versus morality, anarchy versus order, luxury versus austerity, communication versus seduction, and signification versus sensation." Necipoğlu and Payne, eds., *Histories of Ornament: From Global to Local* (Princeton: Princeton University Press, 2016), 5.

3. Robert Levit, "Contemporary Ornament: The Return of the Symbolic Repressed," *Harvard Design Magazine* 28 (Spring/Summer 2008): 2.

4. Farshid Moussavi and Michael Kubo, *The Function of Ornament* (Barcelona: Actar and Harvard University Graduate School of Design, 2006).

5. Moussavi and Kubo, *The Function of Ornament*, 8.

6. Levit, "Contemporary Ornament," 3.

7. Ibid.

8. Hashim Sarkis states that "By leaning on the functional nature of affects, [Moussavi] also aims to reintroduce ornament back into architecture not as excessive or superfluous imagery, but rather as function, maintaining functionalist criteria for acceptance." See Sarkis, "Inscription," in *Histories of Ornament*, 38. Also see Vittoria Di Palma, "A Natural History of Ornament," ibid., 30.

9. Levit, "Contemporary Ornament," 7.

10. Definitions of "ornament" are from www.merriam-webster.com/dictionary/ornament and www.dictionary.com/browse/ornament.

11. This definition from the Roman period is taken from Picon, *Ornament*, 37–39. Picon explains that ornament has been viewed as simultaneously "supported and supporting," neither superficial nor structural but a "necessary supplement."

12. In 1977, a thematic issue of *VIA* was devoted to the topic of ornament. One of the journal's authors, Sir John Summerson, quoted Christopher Dresser's definition from 1862, which used the phrase "superadded to utility." See Summerson, "What Is Ornament and What Is Not," in Stephen Kieran, ed. *VIA: Ornament* 3 (1977): 5. The original quotation is from Dresser, *The Art of Decorative Design* (London: Day and Son, 1862), 1.

13. Kent Bloomer also describes the dual meaning of ornament. See Bloomer, *The Nature of Ornament: Rhythm and Metamorphosis in Architecture* (New York, London: W.W. Norton & Co, 2000), 15.

14. Meyer states that "Beauty is rarely discussed in the discourse of landscape design sustainability and, if it is, dismissed as a superficial concern." See Elizabeth K. Meyer, "Sustaining Beauty: The Performance of Appearance," *Journal of Landscape Architecture* 5 (2008): 30.

15. Ibid, 33.

16. The full quote reads that landscape science is "a systematic study of landscapes themselves, and of processes of landscape-making, in an effort to discern the difference between surface and substance, appearance and essence." Brian Davis and Thomas Oles, "From Architecture to Landscape: The Case for a New Landscape Science," *Places* (October 2014), accessed July 18, 2015, https://placesjournal.org/article/from-architecture-to-landscape/.

17. For an excellent piece on the need for both fiction and function, see Gideon Fink Shapiro, "Simulation and Landscape Fiction," in Karen M'Closkey and Keith VanDerSys, eds., *LA+ SIMULATION* 4 (2016): 6–9.

18. Adolf Loos, *Ornament and Crime* (Riverside, CA: Ariadne Press, 1997), 168. The work was originally written for a lecture in 1910 (though many sources say 1908) and published for the first time in French in 1913. On the confusion surrounding this essay's publication date, see Christopher Long, "The Origins and Context of Adolf Loos's 'Ornament and Crime'," *Journal of the Society of Architectural Historians* 68, no. 2 (June 2009): 200–23.

19. Le Corbusier, *Towards a New Architecture* (New York: Dover Publication, Inc., 1986), 87.

20. With regard to the distinction between ornament and decoration, some describe ornament as the individual element and decoration as the entire field or the effect created through ornament; others prefer to give ornament a higher status by describing it as a "heightening" of its host, whereas decoration is seen more as a superfluous or arbitrary addition. However, most often the terms are used interchangeably, as can be noted by comparing their definitions in various dictionaries. Decoration (décor, decorum) derives from the root form *dek-*, meaning to be suitable or decent. Indeed, both decoration and ornament are inherently bound up with questions of taste and appropriateness. Necipoğlu and Payne note that "The increasing interchangeability of the terms decoration and ornament in the modern period illustrates how the tendency to view it as adjunct (in a supporting role, rather than as its own category) became embedded in language." See Necipoğlu and Payne, *Histories of Ornament*, 5.

21. The quotation is from Jonathan Massey, "Ornament and Decoration," in *Handbook of Interior Architecture and Design*, eds. Graeme Brooker and Lois Weinthal (London: Bloomsbury Academic, 2013), 509. Massey is paraphrasing a statement by German architect Hermann Muthesius from 1902.

22. Christopher Tunnard, *Gardens in the Modern Landscape* (London: Architectural Press, 1948; first printing 1938), 96. For an essay on ornament in relation to the design work of this book's authors, see Karen M'Closkey and Keith VanDerSys, "Not Garden," in *VIA: Dirt*, eds. Megan Born, Helene Furjan, and Lily Jencks (Cambridge: MIT Press and Penn Design, 2011): 284–89.

23. Tunnard, *Gardens in the Modern Landscape*, 96.

24. Ibid, 79.

25. James C. Rose, "Why Not Try Science?" (1939), reprinted in Marc Treib, ed., *Modern Landscape Architecture: A Critical Review* (Cambridge: MIT Press, 1993), 77.

26. James C. Rose, "Plants Dictate Garden Forms" (1938), reprinted in ibid, 72.

27. Many sources describe ornament as present but manifested in less conspicuous ways in modernism. For example, see Thomas H. Beeby, "The Grammar of Ornament/Ornament as Grammar,"

VIA: Ornament 3 (1977), 11–29; Helene Furjan, "Dressing Down: Adolf Loos and the Politics of Ornament," *Journal of Architecture* 8 (2003): 1–16; Caroline Constant, "Adolf Loos and 'The Woman Problem:' Decorum and Modern Architecture," *APPX* 1 (2007): 47–77.

28. Beeby uses examples by Frank Lloyd Wright, Le Corbusier, Mies Van der Rohe, and others to demonstrate how proportioning systems were used to manipulate elements for ornamental purposes.

29. Lars Spuybroek, who argues that Gothic is the most relevant type of ornamental structuring, states that texture is "weak decoration" whereas "strong decoration" makes objects. He states that "this does not mean that ornament literally predates the form or the surface, rather, ornament is abstract making … it recreates the geometrical surface of … a wall abstractly, with rules of growth such as bifurcating, tendriling and the like." Spuybroek, *The Sympathy of Things: Ruskin and the Ecology of Design* (Rotterdam: V2 Publishing, 2011), 129.

30. As with any cultural development, there are many influences and regional variations; however, nature was a primary source of inspiration. For example see, "Art Nouveau 1890-1914," *National Gallery of Art*, accessed November 17, 2015, www.nga.gov/content/dam/ngaweb/ Education/learning-resources/teaching-packets/pdfs/Art-Nouveau-tp.pdf; Peter Kellow, "Vitalism and the Meaning of Art Nouveau," *American Art Quarterly* 30, no. 2 (2013), accessed November 17, 2015, www.nccsc.net/essays/ vitalism-and-meaning-art-nouveau.

31. Anatomist Wilhelm His believed that Haeckel's misrepresentations were tantamount to sinning against objectivity. For the debate between His and Haeckel, see Lorraine Daston and Peter Galison, *Objectivity* (New York: Zone Books, 2007), 191–95.

32. Olaf Breidbach, "Brief Instructions to Viewing Haeckel's Pictures," in *Art Forms in Nature: The Prints of Ernst Haeckel*, eds. Olaf Breidbach and Irenaus Eibl Eibesfeldt (Munich: Prestel, 1998), 16.

33. Martin Kemp, *Seen/Unseen: Art, Science, and Intuition from Leonardo to the Hubble Telescope* (Oxford: Oxford University Press, 2006), 323.

34. James Corner, *The Atlantic*, "First Drafts: James Corner's High Line Park," accessed July 5, 2014, www.theatlantic. com/entertainment/archive/2011/07/

first-drafts-james-corners-high-line-park/240695/.

35. The quotation is from William S. Saunders; within the quotation, the phrase "tyranny of an overriding style" is from Matt Urbanski, one of the firm's principals. Saunders, "The Urban Landscaper: A Second Great Age of City-Making," *Harvard Magazine* (November/December 2013), accessed July 5, 2014, http://harvardmagazine.com/2013/11/the-urban-landscaper.

36. Obviously, not all American landscape architects subscribe to the view that all design moves are "found" in the site. Beginning in the late 1970s and early 1980s, the graphic emphasis of landscape design was evident, most notably in the work of landscape architects Peter Walker, Martha Schwartz, and Ken Smith. All used repetition, a key technique of traditional ornament, while Schwartz and Smith also used garden ornaments (frogs, plastic flowers, etc.); however, they all framed their work as deriving from minimalist or pop art lineages, rather than as attempts to reframe ornament *per se.*

37. An excellent overview of how Bateson's epistemology overcomes the dualism inherent in either subjectivist (sensuous-emotional) or objectivist (rationalist-cognitive) approaches to aesthetics and knowledge is Katja Neves-Graca, "'Aesthetics': Detached Appreciation or Responsiveness to Connection?" (unpublished paper presented at Concordia University, Department of Sociology and Anthropology, North York, Ontario, November 16, 2005). Regarding the possibility of a cause-and-effect relationship between experience and knowledge, Neves-Graca states that her research "shows that this sequence of assumptions does not hold true, because the issue is far more complex—there are many factors at play, such as knowledge and power politics, culturally learned sensitivities, economic goals etc. which make this linear causality impossible."

38. On Bateson's privileging of communicative order over material order in ecology, see Peter Harries-Jones, *A Recursive Vision: Ecological Understanding and Gregory Bateson* (Toronto: University of Toronto Press, 1995), 6.

39. Spuybroek, *The Sympathy of Things,* 291.

40. Gunalan Nadarajan, "Ornamental Biotechnology and Parergonal Aesthetics," in *Signs of Life: Bio Art and Beyond,* ed. Eduardo Kac (Cambridge: MIT Press, 2007), 46.

41. Antoine Picon notes that the type of "pattern[s] that used to play a relatively minor role in the Western ornamental tradition, contrary to the Islamic one, now [appear] as one of the most common forms taken by ornament in contemporary projects." Picon, *Ornament,* 30. However, in *Histories of Ornament,* Necipoğlu and Payne provide a broad geographic and historical overview demonstrating that this characterization of ornament is too simple and does not account for the range of ornamental expressions found within specific cultures.

42. Debra Schafter, *The Order of Ornament, The Structure of Style: Theoretical Foundations of Modern Art and Architecture* (Cambridge: Cambridge University Press, 2003), 30.

43. Describing how ornament came to be distanced from representational values toward more abstraction, Schafter states, "Motifs and the objects with which they were associated interacted through the relationships they established rather than the iconography they created." *The Order of Ornament,* 181.

44. These comments have been heard in our conversations with various other landscape architects, who also stated that the project "looks like Dubai." Similar criticism can be found in various online sources, such as Eikongraphia, "Maple Leaf, by West 8" (2006), accessed July 5, 2014, www.eikongraphia.com/?p=756.

45. Necipoğlu and Payne note that many essays in their book revisit the notion of ornament as a framing device rather than a peripheral element. See *Histories of Ornament,* 5.

46. Kent C. Bloomer and John Kresten Jespersen state that a fundamental characteristic of ornament is "the distribution, by repetition, of a nucleus comprised of a rather small set of basic figures." Ornament-Scholar, "Ornament as Distinct from Decoration," accessed September 29, 2015, http://ornament-scholar.blogspot.com/2014/02/ornament-as-distinct-from-decoration_5274.html.

47. A most striking and celebrated example of nonstructural elements intensifying the expression of structure can be seen in rib vaults. Not all the ribs in late Gothic cathedrals are structurally necessary; however, the added tracery of the nonstructural ribs is inseparable from the structural ribs.

48. This hypothetical student project was located in the Blackwater Estuary in Essex, England. "Slurry #2: Marsh Condenser," *Pruned* (June 14, 2010), accessed July 20, 2014, http://pruned. blogspot.com/2010/06/slurry-2-marsh-condenser.html.

49. Bloomer, *The Nature of Ornament*, 85, describes ornament as the home of metamorphosis. Massey, "Ornament and Decoration," 506, describes the work of Art Nouveau designers such as Hector Guimard, Victor Horta, Louis Comfort Tiffany, and others as evoking "vines, tendrils, and the vital energies coursing through living things."

50. Picon, *Ornament*, 135.

51. Di Palma, "A Natural History of Ornament," 33 and Spuybroek, *The Sympathy of Things*, 98.

52. Spuybroek, *The Sympathy of Things*, 140–41.

53. This excellent characterization is borrowed from Paul Andersen and David Salomon, who state that "a pattern is an organization that a system expands into rather than an underlying structure to which it can be reduced." Andersen and Salomon, *The Architecture of Patterns* (New York: W. W. Norton, 2010), 56.

54. Kubik and Ito's projects are also featured in Karen M'Closkey, "Synthetic Patterns: Fabricating Landscapes in the Age of 'Green,'" *Journal of Landscape Architecture* 15 (2013): 16–27.

55. Necipoğlu and Payne, *Histories of Ornament*, 6.

56. The phrase "consciousness of milieu" is borrowed from Robert Levit, "Design's New Catechism," in *The Return of Nature: Sustaining Architecture in the Face of Sustainability*, eds. Preston Scott Cohen and Erika Naginski (New York: Routledge, 2014), 13.

57. As Picon states, "Contrary to the message conveyed by the founding fathers of modern architecture, from Adolf Loos to Le Corbusier, traditional ornament was not meant solely for pleasure. It conveyed vital information about the purpose of buildings as well as about the rank of the owners. As such, it participated in the expression of social values, hierarchies and order." Picon, *Ornament*, 11.

1. Spyros Papapetros, who is quoted here, is not as critical of this aspect of Kepes's work as others have been. Papapetros argues that "cosmologically-minded architects or historians have also been criticized for their distance from the real, as well as for their allegedly escapist inclination toward a sense of order that is irrevocably lost in the modern world. … [However,] one could argue that … [c]osmology portents a reengagement with the world beyond the limits of its normative periphery, not the reaffirmation of an immutable spatial organization or world order." Papapetros, "MICRO/ MACRO: Architecture, Cosmology, and the Real World," *Perspecta* 42 (2010): 122, 124.

Image Credits

Introduction

Figure 1
Image © James Siena, courtesy of Pace Gallery.

Figure 2
Courtesy of the Land Processes Distributed Active Archive Center (LP DAAC), located at USGS/EROS, Sioux Falls, SD.

Figure 3
Courtesy of NASA/METI/AIST/Japan Space Systems, and U.S./Japan ASTER Science Team.

Figure 4
Courtesy of NASA, ESA, and the Hubble Heritage Team (STScI/AURA).

Figures 5
Courtesy of Mark Nystrom.

Figure 6
© Bridget Riley 2014. All rights reserved, courtesy Karsten Schubert, London.

Figure 7
Courtesy of Emma McNally.

Figure 8
© 2016 The Pollock-Krasner Foundation Artists Rights Society (ARS), New York.

Figure 9
Courtesy of Dr. Dmitri Leonoudakis.

Figure 10
Courtesy of Pedro Miguel Cruz.

Figure 11
Courtesy of Mary Odum. Originally published in *Environment, Power, and Society* (City: John Wiley & Sons Inc., 1971).

Figure 12
Courtesy of iStock.

Figure 13
Courtesy of M. Batty and P. Longley, *Fractal Cities* (Academic Press: San Diego and London, 1994); also at www.fractalcities.org.

Figure 14
Image from *The Complete Works of John Ruskin*, public domain. Originally published in John Ruskin, *Modern Painters*, Vol. 5 (London: Smith, Elder and Co., 1860).

Figure 15
Courtesy of Hyun Chang Cho.

Figure 16
Photograph by Robert Wolstenholme.

Figure 17
Courtesy of Lawrence Halprin Collection, The Architectural Archives, University of Pennsylvania.

Figures 18 and 19
Courtesy of James Corner Field Operations.

Figure 20
Courtesy of Dereck Revington Studio.

Figure 21
Courtesy of Office for Metropolitan Architecture (OMA), Heer Bokelweg 149, 3032 AD Rotterdam, The Netherlands.

Figure 22
Photograph by Wenke Duan.

Figure 23
Photograph by Jonas Bendiksen, courtesy of Magnum Photos.

Figure 24
Courtesy of Northrop Grumman Systems Corporation.

Figures 25 and 26
Courtesy of The Architectural Archives, University of Pennsylvania.

Figures 27 and 28
Courtesy of PWP Landscape Architecture.

Figure 29
Courtesy of Chia-hua Liu.

Figure 30
Courtesy of PEG office of landscape + architecture.

Figure 31
Courtesy of Mark Nystrom.

Chapter 1

Figure 1
Photo by and courtesy of Douglas Moore.

Figure 2
Courtesy of NASA/JPL-Caltech.

Figure 3
Courtesy of Joshua Freese and Jieping Wang.

Figure 4
Courtesy of iStock.

Figure 5
Courtesy of The MIT Media Lab.

Figure 6
Image from A.L. Loeb, *Leonardo* 4, No. 4 (Autumn, 1971): 340. Courtesy of MIT Press.

Figure 7
Image from A.L. Loeb, *Leonardo* 4, No. 4 (Autumn, 1971): 341. Courtesy of MIT Press.

Figure 8
Courtesy of NASA.

Figure 9
Royal Collection Trust/© Her Majesty Queen Elizabeth II 2014.

Figure 10
Photograph by and courtesy of TuAnh Nguyen.

Figure 11
Courtesy of PEG office of landscape + architecture.

Figures 12 and 13
Lawrence Halprin Collection, The Architectural Archives, University of Pennsylvania.

Figure 14
György Kepes, *Flame Orchard*, 1972. Photo: Nishan Bichajian. Courtesy CAVS Special Collection, MIT Program in Art, Culture and Technology. Copyright Massachusetts Institute of Technology.

Figure 15
Photograph from Hans Jenny, *Cymatics: A Study of Wave Phenomena and Vibration* (Basel, Switzerland: Basilius Presse, 1967). Courtesy of © 2001 MACROmedia Publishing, Eliot, ME, USA. www.cymaticsource.com.

Figure 16
Public domain. Image can also be found in Michel Frizot, *Étienne-Jules Marey: Chronophotographe* (Paris: Nathan, Delpire, 2001), 161.

Figure 17
Courtesy of PEG office of landscape + architecture.

Figure 18
Courtesy of Jing Guo.

Figure 19
Courtesy of Freeland Buck.

Figure 20
Courtesy of Edwin Lam and Sean Stevenson.

Figures 21–23
Courtesy of Carlos Ferrater.

Figure 24
Photograph by Sam Holliss.

Figure 25
Courtesy of PEG office of landscape + architecture.

Figures 26 and 27
Courtesy of Elise McCurley, Leeju Kang, Chris Arth.

Figures 28 and 29
Courtesy of PEG office of landscape + architecture.

Figures 30 and 31
Courtesy of Jade Eco Park, 2012–2015, Taichung, Taiwan, Philippe Rahm architectes, Mosbach paysagistes, Ricky Liu & Associates.

Figure 32
Courtesy of Nicholas de Monchaux.

Chapter 2

Figure 1
Courtesy of Juliet K. Stone. Originally
published in György Kepes, *The MIT
Years 1945–1977* (Cambridge: MIT Press,
1978), 33.

Figure 2
Courtesy of NASA.

Figure 3
Courtesy of Dayna Smith.

Figure 4
Walter De Maria, *The Lightning Field*,
1977. Long-term installation, western New
Mexico. © The Estate of Walter De Maria.
Courtesy of Dia Art Foundation, New York.
Photo: John Cliett.

Figure 5
Courtesy of Jasia Reichardt. Reproduced
from *Cybernetic Serendipity* (City:
Frederick A. Praeger, 1968).

Figure 6
Courtesy of Philip Beesley.

Figure 7
Cedric Price fonds, Collection Centre
Canadien d'Architecture/Canadian
Centre for Architecture, Montreal.

Figure 8
Courtesy of Mary Odum. Originally pub-
lished in *Environment, Power, and Society*
(City: John Wiley & Sons Inc., 1971).

Figures 9 and 10
Courtesy of ecoLogicStudio.

Figure 11
Courtesy of Studio Olafur Eliasson.

Figure 12
Courtesy of Sean Lally.

Figure 13
Photograph by and courtesy of Norbert
Aepli, Switzerland.

Figure 14
Courtesy of NASA.

Figure 15
Courtesy of NASA's Goddard Space
Flight Center.

Figure 16
Courtesy of PEG office of landscape +
architecture.

Figures 17 and 18
Courtesy of Michael Ezban.

Figures 19 and 20
Courtesy of David Benjamin and Chris
Woebken.

Figure 21
© 2012 CERN, for the benefit of the ALICE
Collaboration.

Figure 22
Courtesy of Future Cities Lab.

Figure 23
Reprinted with permission of Nokia
Corporation.

Figure 24
Courtesy of National Oceanic and
Atmospheric Administration/Department
of Commerce (NOAA).

Figures 25 and 26
Courtesy of Yusuke Obuchi.

Figure 27
Photograph by and courtesy of Dennis
Hlynsky.

Figure 28
Courtesy of Chris Jordan Studio.

Figure 29
Courtesy of National Oceanic and
Atmospheric Administration/Department
of Commerce (NOAA).

Chapter 3

Figure 1
Image from *Art Forms in Nature: The Prints of Ernst Haeckel*, eds. Olaf Breidbach and Irenäus Eibl-Eibesfeldt (Munich: Prestel, 1998).

Figure 2
Courtesy of Barn Elms Publishing. Originally published in *Knot Gardens & Parterres* (London: Jennings & Whalley, 1998), 75.

Figure 3
Concept, drawings, and video by Matthew Ritchie. In collaboration with Aranda\Lasch, Daniel Bosia and Arup AGU.

Figure 4
Courtesy of Martha Schwartz Partners.

Figure 5
Courtesy of Tom Wiscombe.

Figures 6 and 7
Courtesy of PEG office of landscape + architecture.

Figure 8
Photograph by and courtesy of Marcus Fornell.

Figure 9
Courtesy of Joshua Freese.

Figure 10
Courtesy of Francisco Allard.

Figure 11
Public domain. Image from *Art Forms in Nature: The Prints of Ernst Haeckel*, eds. Olaf Breidbach and Irenäus Eibl-Eibesfeldt (Munich: Prestel, 1998), 9.

Figure 12
Courtesy of the U.S. Geological Survey (USGS).

Figure 13
Courtesy of Laura Splan.

Figure 14
Courtesy of PEG office of landscape + architecture.

Figure 15
Courtesy of Eastman Kodak Company. Published in György Kepes, *The New Landscape in Art and Science* (Chicago: Paul Theobald and Co., 1963; first printing 1956), 9.

Figure 16
Courtesy of Styliane Philippou.

Figure 17
Photograph by Allan Fraga.

Figures 18–20
Courtesy of West 8.

Figure 21
Courtesy of Mecanoo.

Figures 22 and 23
Courtesy of Fabrizio Matillana.

Figures 24–26
Courtesy of Yongjun Jo and Kyung-Kuhn Lee.

Figures 27 and 28
Courtesy of Toyo Ito.

Figures 29–31
Courtesy of Joe Kubik.

Afterword

Courtesy of Iris & B. Gerald Cantor Center for Visual Arts, Stanford University.

Index

Acknowledgments

We would like to express our gratitude to all of the artists, designers, and scientists who granted us permission to use their work and to the Pew Center for Arts & Heritage for awarding us a PEW fellowship that was used in part for image acquisition. Many thanks are due to Marilyn Jordan Taylor, Dean of the School of Design at the University of Pennsylvania, who provided support for book design, and to James Corner for his perennial generosity, both of intellect and time, and for contributing a foreword to our book. At Routledge, we would like to thank Sadé Lee and Louise Fox for their support, assistance, and, most of all, patience. We would like to acknowledge our research assistants, Allison Koll and Brian McVeigh, for the very important task of helping with image permissions. And, lastly, a very special thanks to Caroline Constant and David Salomon for their indispensable insights and generosity of time in reading earlier drafts of the text.

About the Authors

Karen M'Closkey and Keith VanDerSys are faculty members in the Department of Landscape Architecture at the University of Pennsylvania, USA, and founding partners of PEG office of landscape + architecture, a design and research practice based in Philadelphia, USA. Their firm has received numerous design awards and been widely published for its work exploring fabrication technologies in landscape architecture and, most recently, advances in environmental modeling and simulation tools. They are guest editors of the Fall 2016 issue of *LA+* on the topic of simulation. M'Closkey is author of *Unearthed: The Landscapes of Hargreaves Associates* (2013), which won the J. B. Jackson Book Prize from the Foundation for Landscape Studies. She is a Fellow of the American Academy in Rome and was co-recipient with VanDerSys of a 2013 Pew Fellowship in the Arts.